DAN,

THANK YOU FOR

PART OF LISA AND MY

WEDDING DAY.

I HOPE THIS BOOK HELPS

YOU AND YOUR FAMILY DRAW

EVEN NEARER TO OUR LORD.

GOD BLESS.

ROGER

ENGRAVED

ON YOUR

Heart

ENGRAVED

ON YOUR

Heart

Living The Ten Commandments Day By Day

BILL HYBELS

Cook Communications

Victor is an imprint of Cook Communications Ministries,
Colorado Springs, Colorado 80918
Cook Communications, Paris, Ontario
Kingsway Communications, Eastbourne, England

ENGRAVED ON YOUR HEART:
LIVING THE TEN COMMANDMENTS DAY BY DAY
© 1985, 2000 by Bill Hybels. All rights reserved.

Printed in the United States of America

1 2 3 4 5 6 7 8 9 10 Printing/Year 04 03 02 01 00

Unless otherwise noted, Scripture quotations are from the New American
Standard Bible, © the Lockman Foundation 1960, 1962, 1963, 1968, 1971,
1972, 1973, 1975, 1977. Other quotations are from the Authorized (King
James) Version (KJV), The Living Bible (TLB), © 1971, Tyndale House
Publishers, Wheaton, Illinois 60189. Used by permission.

Reflections Writer: Gary Wilde
Cover Design: Peter Schmidt of Granite Design
Interior Design: Peter Schmidt of Granite Design

Library of Congress Cataloging-in-Publication Data
Hybels, Bill.
    Engraved on your heart : living the Ten commandments day by day / Bill
Hybels.
    p.cm.
    ISBN 0-78143-396-7
    1. Ten commandments—Meditations. I. Title.

BV4655 .H9 2000
241.5'2—dc21   00-027208

CONTENTS

Introduction

Ask a hundred people if it's wrong to steal, and ninety-nine will tell you yes. Then ask those ninety-nine if they've ever stolen something, or padded an expense account, or "adjusted" numbers on their tax returns . . . and all ninety-nine of them will probably look down at the ground and nervously shuffle their feet. (So will the one-hundredth one standing off to the side!) In spite of the fog that permeates public discussion of morality, the truth is we all have an internal sense of right and wrong that's remarkably consistent. And we're remarkably consistent violating it.

God gave us ten basic rules about how to relate to Him and others. He wrote them on stone, reproduced them in His Book, and even inscribed them on our hearts. But we continue to have trouble living them out.

These commandments can't save us from sin—only Christ does that—but keeping these commandments saves us from untold heartache and unwanted consequences. God's commandments bring an order to life. When we put Him first, live honorably with family and others, are content with what we have—in other words, do the very things His laws require—life just *works*.

The goal of this book is to provide you with an in-depth look at each of the Ten Commandments. You'll see their importance and why they make sense. Then, it will be up to you. Will you follow God's design for your life? Will you sign on to live out the most important set of instructions ever given to mankind? It's my earnest hope and prayer that you will.

Bill Hybels
Senior Pastor
Willow Creek Community Church

ENGRAVED

ON YOUR

Heart

Choose
The Living God

"You shall have no other gods before Me." Exodus 20:3

This week's devotional theme:

Only God is intrinsically worthy of our
worship and devotion.

Do You Know the Commandments?

Newsweek magazine once reported that only 49 percent of all Protestants, and 44 percent of all Roman Catholics, could name even four of the Ten Commandments! In a seminary class I once taught, I referred to Exodus 20 and casually remarked, "Of course, you all know the Ten Commandments." The empty looks on my students' faces failed to convince me that they did. So I asked if someone—anyone—could name the first commandment. In a class of second-year seminary students, not one student could recite the first commandment!

Yet, someone might fairly ask: Why bother with these ancient statements of the Jewish religion? My response is that, though given by God centuries ago, they continue to have something very important to say to us today. They still have the power to touch our inner lives, and to liberate us from the vices that enslave us and the sins that destroy us.

Moses received these commandments three months after God miraculously delivered the nation of Israel from the land of Egypt. The first four, or the First Table, taught the people how to relate to God. The fifth through tenth commandments, the Second Table, taught them how to relate to one another. If we are willing to take these instructions seriously, they can teach us the same lessons today.

Words of Wisdom

"You shall have no other gods before Me" (Ex. 20:3). With these words, the Almighty God of the Israelites established His rightful position of preeminence. In a historical setting that encouraged devotion to many gods, the God of Israel demanded a single-minded allegiance—to Himself.

Undoubtedly, many of the Israelites questioned Moses on this point, just as some persons question this commandment today. "Was God nervous?" they ask. "Did the competition threaten Him? Why did He have to be so exclusive?"

Those of us who do give our allegiance to the God of the Old Testament would never frame our questions in such blunt terms. But still, we too wonder, "Why did God say this? What were His motives?"

One thing of which we can be sure is that God had good reasons for giving this commandment. The Lord tells us specifically that His commands are never burdensome (1 John 5:3). By this, He doesn't necessarily mean they're easy to keep. Rather, He's telling us that they're never foolish. They are never unnecessary or purely arbitrary. He doesn't force us to observe meaningless formalities, nor does He impose rules that have no value.

The challenge for each of us is to walk closely enough to God, each day, that we might discern how His Words apply to every circumstance we encounter. We can expect His Words—even His commands—to guide us. But first we've got to know what He has said.

Do you know?

Only God Is Worthy

Anyone who has ever witnessed the pathetic sight of human beings bowing down before idols knows why God gave the first commandment in such absolute terms. I once visited a missionary friend in the South American nation of Paraguay. In a little tribal village not far from the capital city of Asunción, we watched as diseased, poverty-stricken villagers fell down on their knees and paid homage to a statue made of chiseled stone. The hopelessness of that scene was indelibly printed on my mind.

I wanted to shout, "Don't waste your worship on that stone! What will it ever do for you?"

The first commandment tells us that no other being in the universe is worthy of our worship. Only Jehovah, the true God of the Bible, deserves our reverence. Why?

Out of all the beings in this universe, only Jehovah God has intrinsic worth. Intrinsic means "belonging to the essence of a thing" or "inherent." In other words, only God has value totally in and of Himself. All else derives its value from association with Him.

That's why we worship Him alone—because of His intrinsic worthship, His creative power, and His redeeming works. In God's prelude to the Law, He identified Himself with these words: "I am the Lord your God, who brought you out of the land of Egypt, out of the house of slavery" (Ex. 20:2).

Before He gave His Law, He wanted to remind the people who He was. "Just a short time ago, you were slaves. You were oppressed. You were humiliated and beaten and deprived. So I sent Moses to lead you to freedom. Then I sent the plagues to assure your release. Then I parted the Red Sea. Then I drowned the Egyptian host. Yes, it was I who delivered you.

"Then I sustained you in the desert. I led you with a fiery cloud when you needed direction. I provided manna and quail when you were hungry. I caused water to flow from the rock when you were thirsty.

"Did Baal do that for you? Did the foreign god, Moleck, do that for you? Did any other gods do that for you? Could they have done it for you? No! I alone had the power to create you, and I alone have the power to sustain you against that which would destroy you. Why would you waste your time worshiping another god?"

When we recognize God's intrinsic worth, we realize how important it is to worship Him, and Him alone. It is not simply for His honor that He demands our worship. He also requires it for our good. He knows that no other being can satisfy the needs and yearnings of our hearts.

During times of grief or disappointment, when it's easy to slip into doubt and confusion, we need a living God, one who can speak to us. We need a God who can give us a word of truth or encouragement or challenge or chastisement. That's the kind of God Jehovah is.

What Consumes Your Thoughts Today?

Several years ago, my brother bought his son Cameron a compass for Christmas. Cam was so thrilled with his gift that he could barely control his excitement. "Hey, Uncle Bill, look what I got from Dad!" he said. "It's a compass. I can shake it up and turn it all around. But when I hold it still again, it always points north."

Our thoughts, too, are always pointing . . . somewhere.

If you're an open-minded person who is devoted to spiritual truth, you've undoubtedly been able to understand and affirm every truth I've stated thus far. You may even have wondered why I've bothered to say it. Am I afraid you're worshiping strange deities? Do I suspect you're bowing down to foreign idols?

In one sense, such thoughts are the farthest things from my mind. I highly doubt that anyone reading this book is involved in the conscious, deliberate worship of gods other than the true God.

In another sense, however, I fear that many well-intentioned Christians have carelessly permitted a multitude of other concerns to become their "gods." They've allowed these concerns to usurp the position of prominence that Jehovah God should have in their affections.

Are you really worshiping the true and living God? Does He have ultimate authority in your life? Is He the chairman of the board? The chief executive officer?

To help you answer those questions honestly, let me ask you another question about your affections: Of whom, or what, do you find yourself thinking during quiet moments of free time?

I realize that most people, including myself, do not have a lot of free thought time. Our thoughts usually are directed toward specific tasks, responsibilities, or conversations—whether we're at home, school, or in the marketplace. But at isolated moments—while we're jogging, driving, waiting in lines, or lying down at night—our minds do have the freedom to focus on whatever we choose.

At such times, where does your mind go? To whom or what do your thoughts automatically turn when they're free to roam?

Our minds, like the needle in that compass, can focus on a variety of subjects throughout the day. But in the end, when they're left alone to settle, they'll focus on the objects of our greatest affection.

Where does your mind settle? On your job? On your girlfriend or boyfriend? On athletic pursuits? On your dream house? On money? On potential accomplishments? On recreation or pleasure?

Please spend a moment contemplating these questions. Your answers probably will reveal the real gods in your life. The person who truly has "no other gods" before the living God usually will find that his thoughts "swing around" until they focus on God. He thinks about God. He meditates on the truths he knows about God. He prays to God. He worships God. Jehovah really is the object of his greatest affection.

Is that experience true for you? Do your thoughts prove that it is?

Whom Are You Trying to Impress?

A close friend from my church once allowed my wife and me to enjoy a winter vacation at his condominium near Palm Springs, California. I started each day of our vacation by jogging through the desert around the condominium complex. The morning air was cool and comfortable and the rising sun softly illuminated the purple mountains in the distance. After running for fifteen or twenty minutes the first morning, the panorama of the surrounding beauty compelled me to kneel in the sand and worship God.

Each morning I returned to that same spot to meditate on all God had done for me and to evaluate my commitment to Him. By the end of the week, I knew I had to renew and verbalize my allegiance to the Lord.

"O God," I prayed, "the last year has come and gone, and now I face a new year. This year I want to worship You and set my affections on You more than I ever did before. I want to strive to please You alone. And I want to pursue the ministry You have given me with heightened passion. I want You to be the God of my life—the ultimate authority."

Can you tell God that?

Where's Your Allegiance?

Year after year after year, we pour our time, energies, and ambitions into a multitude of demanding activities. We study, we work, we save, we buy, we push ourselves, we achieve. And for what? Why do we do it? Whom are we trying to impress? This is another question that can help us determine the real god in our lives.

Some people say they're simply out to impress themselves. They want to do what pleases and satisfies them. They really don't care what anybody else thinks—including God. They're concerned about *their* desires, *their* goals, *their* values. For all practical purposes, they worship themselves. They have become their own god.

People who obey and apply the first commandment, however, learn to be God-pleasers. They are aware of their desires and personal ambitions, but aren't controlled by them. They have close friendships, but they don't allow other people's opinions to dictate their behavior. They want only to impress God.

These people regularly find themselves on their knees, saying, "O God, today I want to be Yours. I want to live according to Your Word. I want Your Spirit to lead me. I want to be obedient. And I don't care what it costs."

Is that prayer your prayer? Or do you bail out if pleasing God might cost you a little pleasure? Or a significant amount of applause?

Take a moment right now to examine your heart and your mind on these matters. Who are you trying to impress?

19

What Are You Living For?

Born into a staunch Dutch Christian Reformed family, I developed the habit of regular church attendance at an early age. Neither threatening weather conditions, tight schedules, nor difficult circumstances would excuse my three sisters, my brother, or me from our usual places in the pew between Mom and Dad.

As is true in most Christian Reformed churches, there came a point in every Sunday morning service when my pastor took on a particularly grave appearance. In a voice that seemed to possess an almost unearthly quality, he'd announce, "And now, beloved, hear the reading of the Law of God. . . ."

When he concluded his reading of Exodus 20—the chapter which contains the Ten Commandments—he read the New Testament summary of the Law: "Thou shalt love the Lord thy God with all thy heart, and with all thy soul, and with all thy mind. . . . And . . . thy neighbor as thyself"(Matt. 22:37-39, KJV). Then, in the same solemn tone, he'd proclaim: "Thus endeth the reading of the Law."

As a child, I had a difficult time coping with this weekly ritual. I always knew exactly what the minister was going to say—in fact, I could have recited the entire passage along with him—so I felt no need to hear it again. Putting my mind on autopilot, I simply endured the repetitious reading without ever considering its real meaning. All I gained from this youthful exercise in endurance was a memorized list of scriptural do's and don'ts.

But there is much more to living than simply memorizing the do's and don'ts. Living for our true and living God involves our life's objectives. We have only one life to live; then we will be called to give an account of what we did with it. When that time comes, what will we have to look back on? What will have been our major objective in life?

Will it have been pleasure? Or the building of an empire? Or the gaining of a position? Or the wielding of power? Will it simply have been to be a "nice guy"?

We have to ask ourselves these questions. What are we trying to accomplish? For what are we living?

The person who understands and obeys the first commandment claims the discovery of God's will as his ultimate objective in life. And he wants not only to discover it, but to pursue it with a passion. He willingly bows before God and implores the Lord to give him a mission in life. "Show me Your will," he prays, "and I'll gladly do it."

If God really is on the throne of your life, your thoughts automatically will turn in His direction, your desire will be to impress Him, and your ultimate objective in life will be to determine His will and do it. If those things are not true in your life, then you're kidding yourself.

You're worshiping a false god.

Week ONE REFLECTIONS

At the end of this week's readings, take some time to think about how these devotionals have affected you. For example, what spiritual insights have you gained? What practical applications have come to mind? How are your attitudes and/or actions likely to change as a result?

Use your responses as "grist" for your journal and as topics for prayer times with the Lord. In this way, you'll keep a record of your spiritual growth as God works out His will in your life.

For Personal Discovery:

1. Why is it actually in your best interest to know, believe, and observe the commandments? The first commandment, in particular?

2. If you were to stand before God today to account for the things or people you made major priorities in life, how would you explain your choices to Him ?

3. What person or thing do you find yourself thinking about in a quiet moment of free time? Why?

4. Consider where you spend your time, money, and energy in a normal day. What does this say about your purpose? About who you are trying to impress?

5. The person who obeys the first commandment wants to pursue God's will with a passion. How are you intentionally seeking to make God's will your ultimate goal? Likewise, in what areas of your life have you let other "gods" compete for your allegiance?

Personal Prayer Focus

- Begin your personal prayer time each day by affirming God's worthiness to receive your total devotion. You might say something like: "I come to You today, Lord, with my joys and concerns because only You have ears to hear my prayers and wisdom to answer them."

- Read and meditate on Job 38 in at least two Bible translations. Listen to what God says about Himself to Job. Then consider: What things do I wish to say to God as a result?

- Offer your praise to God, thanking Him for who He is and how the truth of the first commandment means fullness of life for you.

Journaling My Insights . . .

_____

_____

_____

_____

_____

_____

_____

_____

_____

_____

_____

Week
TWO

Don't Settle
for Shadows

"You shall not make for yourself an idol, or any likeness of what is in heaven above or on the earth beneath or in the water under the earth. You shall not worship them or serve them; for I, the Lord your God, am a jealous God." Exodus 20:4-5

This week's devotional theme:

The reality of God transcends all images and ideas we can possibly conceive of Him.

A Natural Progression?

Scenario: The more you honor God with your obedience and worship, the more God blesses you. That increased blessing prompts in you an even greater desire to obey and worship. Have you noticed? The cycle goes round and round until you join the psalmist and ask, "What shall I render to the Lord for all His benefits toward me?" (116:12)

At this point, the sincere believer must ask himself some questions. Since I have given Him my life, my obedience, my worship, my time, my talents, and my treasures, what more can I do? How can I show Him my appreciation and my adoration?

As the Christian ponders these questions, a new yearning—both exciting and dangerous—begins to grow in his heart. His inner worship begins to plead for an outward expression. He wants to verbalize his love for God and he finds himself singing songs of worship and praise—and enjoying it tremendously! He finds himself praying with greater freedom, intensity, and frequency. He even begins to bow down on his knees as an expression of humility and submission. He wants to show in a tangible way the intangible worship that is welling up in his heart.

His reactions toward God are similar to ones I've experienced toward my kids. There have been times when I'm sitting in the family room reading the newspaper and watching the kids play that I've been overwhelmed with love for them. At such times, I just have to throw the paper aside and grab one of them. "Oh no, it's a love attack!" my daughter happily screams as I pour out my affection in a big bear hug.

Genuine love calls out for expression; and as the intensity of that love grows, the desire to express it in increasingly tangible forms also grows. So it is that over the course of history, believers who were filled with love for God began to feel that desire to give tangible form to their worship. They wanted to facilitate and enhance their devotion by focusing on objects that would attract their attention and call them to worship.

That desire seems innocent enough, doesn't it? On the surface it seems harmless, even commendable. And yet, in the face of that natural and overwhelming desire, God says, "No graven images. No likeness of anything that is in heaven above, earth beneath, or in the water under the earth. No worship helpers."

Why is this? Is God being unreasonable? Does He question our motives? What was going through His mind when He gave that commandment?

I think the answer is obvious. No image constructed by human hands could ever accurately represent the totality, the transcendency, and the majesty of God. We could never shape, paint, or chisel anything that would be an adequate representation of who God is. To attempt to do so would be like asking a scholar to explain the history of the world in one sentence, or a sculptor to make a replica of Mount Rushmore on a single grain of sand, or a musician to play Beethoven's Fifth Symphony with a referee's whistle. It just can't be done. It's absurd even to suggest it!

More Than a Golden Calf

It's a tragic irony that while God was giving Moses the second commandment, the nation of Israel was engaged in the very activity that it forbids. Exodus tells us that during Moses' extended stay on the mountain, the people began to doubt he would ever return to lead them. As a result, they decided to "make a god" that could go on before them. Aaron, their leader during Moses' absence, gathered together gold jewelry from the people, melted it down, and fashioned it into a golden bull. Then he built an altar before it and said, "Tomorrow shall be a feast to the Lord" (32:5).

Why the Idol?

While some commentators believe that in building their golden calf the Israelites abandoned the true God, others believe they had no such intention. Aaron's declaration of a feast "to the Lord" seems to indicate that he, at least, had not turned to another god. He was simply yielding to the people's request for a tangible image of their God. As commentator Robert Jamieson noted: "They required, like children, to have something to strike their sense . . . some visible material object as the symbol of the Divine presence, which should go before them." In other words, if the Israelites couldn't have their visible, human leader, Moses, at least they would have a portrayal of a God that they could see, touch, and display.

But God was offended. So offended, in fact, that only Moses' impassioned plea for mercy kept the Lord from destroying the nation altogether.

Why the Anger?

Why was God so intensely angered? Because He knew that a bull—or any other tangible symbol—could portray only a minuscule portion of His true character. Yes, the bull portrayed His power; but what of His holiness, His majesty, His love? Could it be that their imitation of Egyptian ceremony blinded their eyes to the mystery of God's absolute moral perfection?

You see, the Israelites meant the calf to be an image of the true God, so they were not violating the first commandment—only the second. In other words, they didn't turn to a false god—they merely made an image of the real God.

Can it happen to you and me today? Yes—and it can be our downfall! Why? Because like all images, the thing we cling to as a divine representation will be unable to portray the fullness of God's identity. As a result, it will hinder rather than help our worship. It will lead us down the crooked path of disobedience.

The Creator: Bigger than Creation

The idolatrous sin of the Israelites is obvious. But let's go a little deeper into what all of this has to do with us. What do the ancient story and the second commandment have to do with contemporary Christians who clearly know better than to create a golden calf?

To answer that question, I'm going to have to "tiptoe through a minefield." I realize I'll probably detonate a few bombs and catch a little shrapnel along the way; but this journey must be made if you and I are to be sensitive to the implications of God's commandment.

In my opinion, some modern-day images and objects ought to be evaluated carefully in the light of this commandment. For example, many people, particularly those brought up in the Roman Catholic tradition, give the crucifix an honored place in the vast array of religious symbols. Picturing Jesus on the cross, in pain and agony dying for the sins of the world, the crucifix is a graphic portrayal of the greatest act of love ever demonstrated on this planet. It reminds us of a real event that is precious to all true believers. What could possibly be wrong with praying in the presence of a crucifix or attaching a value to it?

The problem, says J. I. Packer in his book *Knowing God*, is that the crucifix highlights Jesus' human weakness without conveying His divine strength. It depicts the reality of His pain and suffering, but fails to remind us of His victory and joy. It shows us a dying Jesus, but neglects to show us a living Jesus bursting forth from the tomb with resurrection power.

I have no problem with what the crucifix depicts, only with what it fails to depict. It fails to give us an accurate picture of the totality of who our God is. It conveys only a fraction of His true identity.

Perhaps you're thinking, "Come on, give it a break. An image can't convey everything." That's exactly my point! Images can't convey everything. So God says, "Don't try. Don't use them. They can't do the job!"

For example, why should we hang a cross and not portray the empty tomb? Or why an empty tomb and not a manger? The miracle of Jesus' incarnation is as central to our faith as is His death or resurrection. The fact that Jesus, being totally God, also became totally man, is the truth from which our faith derives its significance.

And what about pictures of Jesus? The Jesus of the '60s looked like a campus radical, a fitting leader for a revolutionary age. In the '70s we had a macho Jesus, perfectly proportioned and well-groomed, the obvious creation of a narcissistic society. How will we picture Him in upcoming decades? Will we squeeze Him into the mold of the young, upwardly mobile middle class? What image of Jesus will please us most and make Him acceptable?

In other words, which single emblem can accurately portray the totality of who God is or what Jesus Christ has done for you? None of them can. That's why I'm urging you to avoid attaching yourself to any image at all. If art—shapes and colors and music—help you to worship in spirit and in truth, all well and good. Just beware the danger in thinking that you could ever grasp the fullness of the Creator by holding to a small piece of what He's created.

Buddy Up to the Almighty?

Scripture calls us to worship in spirit and in truth (John 4:24). That is, we must worship the God who really exists, rather than a figment of our imagination. That's why we go to the Bible to bask in the multifaceted light of His divine character.

But people who ignore the written, revealed truth about God inevitably end up with a distorted view of Him. Many people, even Christians, perceive God as a tightfisted judge. Yet the Bible tells us that God is no anxious ogre; His first choice is to win us by His love (see John 3:17). Some people see God as a military general, coldly barking out orders and issuing ultimatums, but they've forgotten that the God of Scripture encourages His children to call Him "Abba, Father," which means "Daddy" (Rom. 8:15-16). Others view God as the actor George Burns portrayed Him in the movies—a funny old man in tennis shoes and glasses. God is their buddy, a nice guy to have around.

Not long ago on a flight to California I sat next to a girl who told me she was living with her boyfriend, had a drinking problem, and frequently used cocaine. She made casual references to other aspects of her lifestyle that were both illegal and immoral. Finally, the conversation turned to Christianity.

"How do you square your lifestyle with God's will, His wisdom, and His Word?" I asked her.

Without giving it a second thought, she responded with the kind of sentiment voiced all too frequently these days: "Well, my God is the grandfatherly type, who loves me and takes care of me and tells me I'm okay. He knows that boys will be boys and girls will be girls. He doesn't care much what I do."

It's so much easier for us to change God than it is to conform to His will. Who wants to face the expectations of a Holy God when they can create a metaphysical grandfather who will pat them benignly on the head and ignore their sin? Who wants an accurate image of a sovereign God when they can create a convenient image that never interferes with their selfish desires?

Yet we can't just buddy up to God on our own terms. The real God of Scripture is more than a pal. When Isaiah experienced his life-changing vision of the Almighty, he didn't quip, "Hey, God, nice to see You. I've been looking forward to this for a long time. You're a real sport." Instead he said, in effect, "Woe is me, for I am a sinful man. How can I survive in the presence of a holy God?" (Isa. 6:5)

Will that be your own attitude in His presence today? Remember: Erroneous mental images are as loathsome to God as the Israelites' golden bull. The second commandment prohibits them as clearly as any material image created by human hands.

Instead of Shadows: Substance!

You've never been one to fashion heathen idols, right? But if you're like me, you've probably found that the second commandment sneaks up on you rather unsuspectingly, now that you've given it some serious consideration.

Let me show you what I mean. I recently received a phone call from a man who said he had visited our church and was very troubled because I preached from a clear-plastic pulpit. For my benefit, he explained the tradition behind the wooden pulpit, and wondered how I possibly could justify deviating from that accepted form. After a lengthy conversation, we cordially agreed to disagree. Still, I was saddened by the fact that we spent half an hour discussing pulpit construction without even once discussing what I proclaimed from it.

How typical that is of the human mind! We focus on wood and plastic when we should be focusing on the spiritual truths so compellingly revealed in God's Word. We place undue importance on shadows and neglect the substance of the Christian faith.

You see, the point I've been making throughout this week of devotions is that God knows that any image we might use to portray Him or "enhance His image" would depict Him as less than He truly is. Whether we use wood or glass, steel or plastic, our creation would reduce His power, His character, and His mysterious holiness. Eventually, we probably would begin to conceive of Him in ways that mirrored the image we constructed, rather than as the mighty God of Scripture. We would end up worshiping not Him, but merely a shadow of who He really is. And He doesn't want us to dishonor Him or waste our time by worshiping a shadow.

The church is called to give people more than a creed, a ceremony, a tradition, a formula, or a shadow. The body of Christ has the matchless privilege and awesome responsibility of giving people what they yearn for in their hearts—truth that will lead them to a daily, dynamic, life-changing relationship with a living Savior. We all need to understand that if we repent of our sins and follow Jesus Christ, we will have a vital relationship with a living God whom we can worship anywhere, anytime.

How I pray that the church of the twenty-first century will be freed from the tyranny of dusty relics that can never represent the totality of our almighty God! May we learn to worship God in spirit and in truth. May we refuse to settle for convenient images, and instead pursue with diligence a greater knowledge of the one true God.

Will you commit yourself to doing that?

Week TWO REFLECTIONS

At the end of this week's readings, take some time to think about how these devotionals have affected you. For example, what spiritual insights have you gained? What practical applications have come to mind? How are your attitudes and/or actions likely to change as a result?

Use your responses as "grist" for your journal and as topics for prayer times with the Lord. In this way, you'll keep a record of your spiritual growth as God works out His will in your life.

For Personal Discovery:

1. On a religious continuum (highly sacramental traditions being to the far left of the spectrum and traditions that renounce all use of imagery representing the far right), where would you place yourself, and why? How do you conceive of God? For example, what does God "look like" to you?

2. Read Exodus 20:4-6. God does not want us to make images of Him because no one image can adequately reflect God's nature in all its fullness. What do you think about "aids" to worship? Are all images "idols"?

3. Read John 4:21-24. What does it mean for you to worship God "in spirit and truth"? How can images actually prevent spiritual and truthful worship?

4. Christians can worship God anywhere—on top of a mountain, while driving the car, on a walk at the beach. In view of this, what do you think about the use of certain places or items such as a sanctuary, stained glass windows, or incense to enhance your ability to worship God?

Personal Prayer Focus

- Take time to confess to God any misrepresentations of Him you have been cultivating.

- Ask the Holy Spirit to help you understand God's nature more fully as you meditate on Scripture's revelation of Him.

- End your prayer time by naming some of the images of God provided in Scripture, thereby affirming His true character. You might pray: "Lord Jesus, I thank You that You are the Good Shepherd who. . . ."

Journaling My Insights . . .

_____

_____

_____

_____

_____

_____

_____

_____

_____

_____

_____

_____

Week THREE

Turn Profanity Into Praise

"You shall not take the name of the Lord your God in vain, for the Lord will not leave him unpunished who takes His name in vain." Exodus 20:7

This week's devotional theme:

The name of God expresses His being and His holiness.

Take Care with Those Words!

Pretend you're in a restaurant, quietly minding your own business; suddenly, the person in the booth behind you says something you just can't help but overhear. As you mull over the brief bit of conversation you've overheard, you think, *Ah, I know what that person does for a living.* You may have heard: "Spec buying has pretty much squeezed the shorts out of the action." And you know you've been listening to a stockbroker.

Certain other kinds of words and phrases are clear tip-offs, too. They may not tell us about the occupations of the speakers, but they do indicate something very important about their inner lives. When we hear someone use the names of God or Jesus Christ as obscenities—or as convenient expressions of anger, frustration, or fear—we know immediately that they have not yet had a real glimpse of the majesty, holiness, and wonder of God.

The first commandment tells us we need to have the right God on the throne of our lives. The second commandment counsels us to make sure we really are worshiping Him, and not just a shadow of who He is. The third commandment now tells us that even His name is to be held in honor and respect. Every time we utter God's name, or sing it, we must do so thoughtfully. We should never use His name frivolously or mechanically, and it goes without saying that we should never use it profanely.

Tim Vandenbos, the director of our church camp, used to have a German shepherd named Jesse, which he bought while serving in the Army overseas. Stationed in a guard tower for long stretches of time without human companionship, Tim developed a warm relationship with his dog. Naturally, the dog developed an intense loyalty to Tim.

Years later, at our camp in upper Michigan, Jesse still followed Tim everywhere. They separated only when Tim had to go down the river for supplies. Then Jesse would lie on the dock, ears drooping and sick at heart, to await Tim's return. Some of the camp workers who knew of Tim's relationship with his dog occasionally walked down to the beach to have a little fun.

"Hey, Jesse," they would taunt, "where's Ralph?" Jesse would not respond.

"Hey, Jesse," they would try again, "where's Joe?" Still no response.

"Hey, Jesse, where's Tim?" At that point, Jesse would go wild! His ears would perk up, his tail would wag, and he'd start running back and forth along the beach, hoping to hear the sound of Tim's returning boat. The mere mention of Tim's name awakened Jesse's feelings of affection for him. A single word brought his master to mind.

So it is when we hear, speak, or sing the name of God. Immediately, the truths we know about the One behind that name come into our minds. The third commandment tells us that when such thoughts occur, we'd better be prepared to worship—for the Being who comes to mind is the intrinsically worthy God who created and sustains us, and who gives us hope for the future.

Does It Really Matter to God?

We read in Leviticus that the son of an Israelite woman got into a scuffle with another man. During the course of the fight, the Israelite "blasphemed the Name and cursed" (24:11). In ancient Israel, there was no doubt as to which "Name" was so revered that its use as a curse constituted blasphemy. Only one name was so honored—the name of God.

Unfortunately for him, some men who knew the commandments of God heard the man's blasphemous curse. After the fight they took him before Moses and asked Moses what should be done with someone who cursed the Name. Moses communicated God's answer: "Stone him."

In effect, God was saying, "What right does a sinner have to shake his little fist in anger and blaspheme the name of the holy God? That is the height of audacity. It just can't be tolerated!"

"But," you may say, "that was during Old Testament times. Things have changed since then. What does the New Testament say?"

As a matter of fact, Jesus did have something very important to say about God's name. To feel some of its impact, join me in another little exercise in creative thinking. Imagine that Jesus came to your church one Sunday morning, wanting to share from the pulpit His most important prayer concerns with you. Do you have any doubts about how you'd respond to His quietly spoken, "Please listen carefully"? Of course not! You, and every true believer in that sanctuary, would grab a pencil and paper as fast as you could and wait in eager anticipation. The very Son of God, the Savior, was going to share the greatest concerns of His heart with you. What an honor! What a privilege!

That imaginary situation closely mirrors the circumstances surrounding Jesus' teaching of the Lord's Prayer. When Jesus' disciples asked Him how to pray, He responded by giving them an adaptable pattern for prayer—and a glimpse into His own prayer life.

"Our Father who art in heaven," He began, "hallowed be Thy name" (Matt. 6:9). After clearly establishing the identity of the One to whom He prayed, He immediately expressed His number one concern—that God's name be hallowed. He wanted it to be reverenced and honored and used only in a way that would bring God glory.

Can we doubt God's seriousness about how we use His name? My friend, will you watch your tongue today, as I attempt to do the same?

Uninformed? No Excuse!

I have no trouble relating to the idea that some people break the third commandment out of sheer ignorance. My father ran a wholesale produce company that his father had founded. When I was in second grade, Dad started taking me to the warehouse on Saturday mornings, where I learned a few things from the dockworkers there—including some four-letter words that I didn't even understand.

One Saturday afternoon, after returning from the warehouse, I was in my bedroom with my older brother, Dan, who had always made it clear that he considered me a real loser. Nothing I did ever impressed him or made him proud of me. Everything I did was minor-league kid stuff . . . until that particular Saturday afternoon.

Welcome to the Big Leagues!

As usual, we were in my room, when I blurted out a new word I had learned from the dockhands. Boy, was Dan surprised—and impressed. He stared at me with eyes as big as saucers, and I could tell he thought that was just about the neatest thing I had ever said. I went from the minor leagues to the majors. Dan smiled as if to say, "You're really something, Billy. You've got guts for a little guy!"

At dinnertime, Mom, Dad, and all five of us kids sat around the big kitchen table the way we always did, a perfect picture of a nice, Norman Rockwell family. Near the end of the meal, my dad asked what Dan and I were going to do after dinner. Leaning back in my chair, I jauntily cocked my head to the side and casually said one of my newly acquired words—the way I'd heard the dockhands say it to express an "I don't care" attitude.

I looked at Dan to catch his smile, but for some reason he wasn't smiling. On the contrary, he looked horror-stricken. As my eyes darted around the table, I saw that my older sister was gasping for air, my mother was starting to cry, and my dad was slowly backing out of his chair, coming my way. I knew then that I'd been had.

Back to the Minors

All the way down the hall to my bedroom I begged for mercy. "Dad, I didn't know. Dan tricked me. He thought it was cool. I didn't know. I didn't know. I didn't . . ."

I honestly didn't know that the word was a problem. In my naivete, I thought anything so commonly used and so obviously impressive had to be all right. I was genuinely ignorant of the truth.

Perhaps you have slipped into the careless use of God's name. After all, it's commonly used in school, in the marketplace, in the neighborhood. Perhaps you have been unaware, though, that this is a grievous sin—a sin so serious that in the Old Testament it led to death. In this matter there is no room for ignorance.

If you have dishonored God's name in ignorance, I challenge you right now to implore His forgiveness and commit yourself to obedience. Decide right now that you're never going to profane His name again.

Not Ignorant, Just Uncontrolled

Some people profane God's name because they don't know any better; others do so simply because they can't control their tongues. Of course, the Bible openly acknowledges the difficulty of this. Scripture tells us that every species of beast, bird, reptile, and sea animal can be tamed by the human race; but no one can control the human tongue (James 3:7-8). Yet God says that we must control it.

We can begin by examining our hearts. Jesus said, "The good man out of the good treasure of his heart brings forth what is good; and the evil man out of the evil treasure brings forth what is evil; for his mouth speaks from that which fills his heart" (Luke 6:45).

Jesus is saying here that neither good intentions nor self-discipline can keep us from losing control of our tongues if there's sin in our hearts. When the pressure is on, the rebellion—or bitterness, anger, or hatred—that's hidden in the recesses of our inner lives will erupt into an explosion of profanity. The only sure way to clean up our mouths, then, is to clean up our hearts.

Fortunately, we don't have to clean up our hearts alone; the Holy Spirit will help us. We begin by asking for His divine intervention. The Holy Spirit is no tyrant who imposes His work on us against our will. He waits to be invited. So we begin with an invitation. We ask Him to clean the sin out of our hearts, and then fill us with the fruit of His Spirit—love, joy, peace, patience, kindness, goodness, faithfulness, gentleness, and self-control (Gal. 5:22-23).

We can cooperate with the work of the Holy Spirit by diligently obeying the first and second commandments. That involves yielding to God's authority and realizing that He's more than just a convenient image based on human opinions. He's the holy God of Scripture who deserves our humble adoration.

We also can support the work of the Holy Spirit in our lives by reading the Bible, listening to Christian music, and having spiritually-oriented conversations with other believers. The more we saturate our minds with the knowledge of God's holiness and majesty, the less likely we'll be to profane His name. We'll gradually find that profanity rarely comes to mind. If it does, the thought of dishonoring God's name will be appalling. We won't even be tempted to do it.

Who's in Charge?

For the first twelve months after my father died, I couldn't stand to hear undertaker jokes. When somebody said, "Hey, did you hear the one about the funeral director?" I just wanted to say, "Please, stop. I don't want to hear about that. It's not funny to me."

Similarly, those who have been pierced with the knowledge of their sin find no humor in careless talk that profanes the name of the One who has loved and redeemed them. They have come face-to-face with the fact that someday they are going to stand before a holy God. When they do, their good works, their money, their power, their talents, and their accomplishments are going to mean nothing. They'll stand before God empty-handed—unless they repent of their sins and ask Jesus Christ to be their Lord.

So they do that. As a result, they begin to feel a deep sense of peace and assurance. They know they've been forgiven and offered the hope of eternal life. This motivates them to love and worship the Lord. Eventually, they find that the name of Jesus has become precious to them, that the name of God has become a word to be revered. The last thing they want to do is profane those names.

In contrast, there are some people who feel no remorse when they flagrantly violate the third commandment. These people are a flashing neon sign that says, "I'm in charge here. I'm the boss!" They're like the teenager who smokes in front of his mom and dad for the first time. For months he's been hiding in alleys and other people's cars, smoking on the sly. Then one day he walks into the family room, lights up, takes a long drag, and looks his parents straight in the eyes. In effect, he's announcing, "You don't scare me anymore. You have no control over me. I don't care what you think or how you feel."

Unbelievers who profane God's name are saying essentially the same thing. And some of them have been saying it for thirty, forty, even fifty years. Are you one of those people? Are you someone who flaunts your profanity in the face of God?

If so, the good news is that the same God you've been cursing loves you. Right this minute He's waiting to open His arms and embrace you as His child. All you have to do is repent. Just say, "Lord, I'm the one with the filthy mouth—the one who's been cursing Your name. I'm the one who's been shaking my puny little fist in rebellion. And now I'm sorry. I ask for Your forgiveness. I don't want Jesus Christ to be my favorite curse word. I want Him to be my Savior."

You see, the Lord of the universe is head over heels in love with you. Though you may have cursed the name of the One who spilled His blood for you, God still says, "Come. Repent. Be My child."

Doesn't that make you want to offer God a heart that's pure and lips that honor His name?

Week THREE REFLECTIONS

At the end of this week's readings, take some time to think about how these devotionals have affected you. For example, what spiritual insights have you gained? What practical applications have come to mind? How are your attitudes and/or actions likely to change as a result?

Use your responses as "grist" for your journal and as topics for prayer times with the Lord. In this way, you'll keep a record of your spiritual growth as God works out His will in your life.

For Personal Discovery:

1. Read Genesis 17:4-5 and 32:28. Why did God change the names of these people?

2. Read Hosea 1:3-9 and Matthew 1:21. How did God use the names of these people for a purpose?

3. Every time we utter God's name, or sing it, we must do so thoughtfully. What would be your greatest difficulty in following this standard? Why is it wrong to misuse God's name?

4. Paul, in Colossians 3:17, exhorts Christians to strive to please God in everything they say. Should there then be any difference between how you use God's name and other things that you say, or are they all somehow related?

5. What are some ways you misuse God's name both directly (as in active rebellion) and indirectly (as in ignorance)?

6. In the Lord's Prayer (Matt. 6:9), Jesus instructs His disciples to "hallow" God's name. Make a list of some practical ways that you can hallow God's name. Which of these is a reasonable next step in your walk with Christ?

Personal Prayer Focus

- Make it a regular part of your prayer time to ascribe to God some of the names given to Him in the Bible. You might begin your time of prayer by saying something like: "O God, You are the Creator of the universe and the Sustainer of all living things. . . ."

- Read 2 Timothy 2:11-13. Confess your sins against God's name, asking for His Spirit to change you. Thank Him that, as we desire to be more like Him, He remains faithful to us because we are His.

- Choose a mature Christian friend and ask him or her to hold you accountable to make and to keep God's name holy in the fullest sense of this commandment.

Journaling My Insights . . .

_____

_____

_____

_____

_____

_____

_____

_____

_____

_____

Week FOUR

Follow The
Maintenance Schedule

"Remember the sabbath day, to keep it holy. Six days you shall labor and do all your work, but the seventh day is a sabbath of the Lord your God; in it you shall not do any work, you or your son or your daughter, your male or your female servant or your cattle or your sojourner who stays with you. For in six days the Lord made the heavens and the earth, the sea and all that is in them, and rested on the seventh day; therefore the Lord blessed the sabbath day and made it holy." Exodus 20:8-11

This week's devotional theme:

God has established the day of rest as a time of physical, emotional, and spiritual refreshment for His people.

More to Life Than Labor

A member of my church owns and drives an airport limousine for a living. As he was taking my wife and me to the airport several weeks ago, I asked him how many miles he thought he would get out of his limo. He told me he had driven his previous vehicle over 400,000 miles without a single major engine repair, and he fully expected to do the same with his current one.

I was dumbfounded. "How can you possibly put that many miles on a car?"

He answered with a single word: "Maintenance."

Want Optimal Performance?

Maintenance is the key to more than optimal car performance. It's also essential to optimal human performance. And if a car needs an owner's manual to define proper maintenance, so do we. Fortunately, we have one—the Bible. One of the many benefits that this owner's manual provides is a "Maintenance Law"—the fourth commandment—which tells us how to maintain a level of peak performance in our lives through a wisely designed upkeep schedule.

God begins the fourth commandment with a positive statement—"Remember the sabbath day, to keep it holy"—and clarifies it with a negative statement—"In it you shall not do any work." Then, as if He anticipates our resistance to this simple command, He silences us with a refresher course on the sequence of Creation.

Genesis 1 tells us that on the first day God called forth light, and separated the day from the night. On the second day

He created the vast expanse of sky called "the heavens." On the third day He caused the dry land to appear and covered it with vegetation. On the fourth day He created the sun, the moon, and the stars. On the fifth and sixth days He filled the earth with animals. Then, finally, He created man. From the dust of the ground He formed him, and breathed into his nostrils the breath of life.

During six distinct periods of time, God moved from the most basic elements of creation to the most phenomenally complex. So what now, we wonder. What's left for Him to do on the seventh day?

Take Time Out

Genesis tells us that "by the seventh day God completed His work which He had done; and He rested on the seventh day from all His work which He had done. Then God blessed the seventh day and sanctified it, because in it He rested from all His work which God had created and made" (2:2-3).

Obviously, God was not trying to illustrate His personal fatigue. He was, instead, introducing a maintenance plan for the human race. He was so serious about this principle of maintenance, in fact, that He chose to use Himself as an example. He wanted to announce to all creation, and all history, that after six days of labor, enough is enough! Labor is a very good thing—but it's not the only thing. There is more to life than labor.

A Necessary Break

God told us 3,000 years ago what production analysts have concluded only recently: that reasonably spaced and carefully used work breaks clearly increase productivity. Statistics show that after approximately forty hours of work, concentration levels drop, mistakes increase, and morale takes a nosedive. Even one's health is affected. Doctors tell us that workaholics (those seven-day-a-week workers who mock God's plan) lead the charts in work-related disorders such as high blood pressure and premature heart attacks. If we refuse to cease from our labors on a regular basis, we inevitably will experience the telltale signs of breakdown.

God knew that all along, so He built a work break right into the system—a one-day minivacation, so to speak—a time for our bodies to recuperate.

For Your Emotions Too!

In this technologically oriented society, few people experience the physical stress of battered muscles and calloused skin. Many, however, experience the emotional stress that accompanies a schedule filled with too many people and too many demands. They grow weary of phone calls, memos, printouts, appointments, interviews, classes, meetings, forms, credit checks, and deadlines. By 5 P.M. on Friday, they're emotional casualties. They start making poor decisions, thus jeopardizing profits. They become short and antagonistic, thus jeopardizing relationships. And everyone around them, in the workplace and at home, can tell they need exactly what God says they need—a break. We may have to make some exceptions because of the nature of our work or service, but we should never make the exceptions lightly.

An unusually strong Christian influence permeated the small town in which I grew up. Because of that influence, any place of business that remained open on Sunday was doomed to fail. The Christians in town simply would avoid that restaurant, store, or shopping center. Within six weeks it would be out of business—unless, of course, the proprietor promptly posted a "Closed on Sunday" sign!

The growth of that town, and the accompanying demise of its Christian influence, led to a dramatic revision of the unofficial code of Sabbath day observance. Today, many local businesses are open on Sunday. For many years, though, the people of that community held to a very important principle. They knew that for one day each week, they had to stop working, and allow themselves to be refreshed physically and cleansed emotionally.

Do you hold to this principle in your personal life? If not, what is keeping you so busy that there's no time to refresh yourself with the rest God clearly desires for you? Why overburden yourself when He invites you to lay down your load—at least for one day per week?

The Flip Side: Worship

There is more to the Sabbath than the absence of labor. There's also the presence of worship.

The Old Testament Israelites gathered for Sabbath day worship at the tent of meeting, and later, at the tabernacle. Jesus, too, went to the local synagogue to worship on the Sabbath, "as was His custom" (Luke 4:16). We also see this pattern of worship continued in the early church. After Jesus' resurrection, the Sabbath was changed from the last day of the week to the first. But the change in day signaled no change in purpose. Early Christians still knew that on the Sabbath they had to stop working and start worshiping.

The author of Hebrews says, in no uncertain terms, that we should not neglect corporate meetings of the church (10:25). Why did God so clearly establish the priority of these weekly gatherings? I think it's because He knew how badly we would need to be chastened, challenged, and changed on a regular basis.

When I stand before my congregation on Sunday mornings, I feel like a doctor performing open-heart surgery. That brief hour and fifteen minutes on Sunday morning is the only time some people open their hearts to the truths of God's Word. For just a little while, they drop the defenses they've hidden behind during the week, and allow God to touch and change their hearts.

The stakes of physical open-heart surgery are weighty—life and death. But those stakes seem inconsequential when we enter the realm of the spiritual. The stakes of spiritual heart surgery are eternal life and eternal death. Some people wonder why I give my Sunday messages with such passion. It's because I know what the stakes are. How can a minister take the message of eternal destiny lightly? How can anyone take it lightly?

We all need to cease from our labors on Sunday and gather together for open-heart surgery. Some people need major surgery. They need to address such crucial issues as sin and death and eternity. Others need minor surgery, repair work. They need a time for confession and challenge. But in one way or another, we all need this time of rest.

We also can benefit from the weekly change that corporate meetings offer. First, we need a physical change. We need to get out of the office, the truck, the school, the plant, the store—out of the place where we perform our labor. We need a new environment, where we can rub shoulders with different people.

We also require an emotional change. We need to hear different language patterns and music. We need to be caught up in a different value system.

We need to encounter joy and creativity and meaning.

And, of course, we need a spiritual change. We need to attend a church where God's Word is believed and taught without apology. We need a pastor who doesn't gloss over important issues or trade truth for personal opinions and vain speculations. We need solid, biblical information.

Don't Just Sit

Sometimes on Sunday mornings, when I look out over my congregation, I can sense the work of the Spirit. I can tell that by God's grace, people are being nurtured and challenged. It's tremendously exciting to see that. Yet a nagging question often haunts me. How long will this spiritual meal last? How long before its nourishing effect wears off?

I know that in less than twenty-four hours, most of these congregants are going back into a secular marketplace, school, or neighborhood. There's a good chance that after three or four days back in the world, even the strongest Christian will need another spiritual meal. After six or seven days, there's no question about it. It's high time to replenish the food supply and refocus spiritually.

God knows the inevitable rhythms of our lives. He knows that if we work seven days a week, week after week, we'll begin to lose perspective on the true meaning of life. We'll get to the point where all we care about are bigger barns, more deals, and higher yields. We'll be worn out physically, burned out emotionally, and out of touch with spiritual realities. We'll be caught in a downward spiral that weakens our marriages, our families, our friendships, our health, and even our moral convictions.

But God says, "Hey, I know you and I love you, and I don't want that to happen to you. So quit working! Take a break! Get recharged!"

It's so important for us to attend churches where we can really grow. Recently, a man told me he used to walk to a church two minutes from his home, twice every Sunday, but still was feeling spiritually malnourished. Now he drives forty-five minutes to a different church. There he's alive, growing, and excited about his faith! For him, a forty-five minute trip was the key to his spiritual life; it took him from a church that didn't meet his spiritual needs to one that did.

What about you? Are you attending a church that recharges you spiritually? Many times I've told members of my congregation that if they're not being fed spiritually at our church, they should go elsewhere. If they don't respect their leaders, if they can't understand the teaching, if there's no place for them to get involved, then they should find a more suitable church.

Several years ago I was the chaplain for the Chicago Bears football team. Occasionally, benched players told me of their frustrations about not playing. They even shared their fantasies of grabbing the coach and saying, "Hey, if I'm not going to play, just tell me! Let me go to a team where I can play. I want to make a difference. I want to use my skills."

Most of us probably feel just like those football players. We want to contribute. We want to work. We want to be starting members of the team. The good news is that in a properly functioning church, we can be—and should be. If that's not true in your church, perhaps you should find a church where there's more of an opportunity to serve.

Enjoy—and Never Stand Alone

Jesus tells us that the Sabbath was created for man's good, and not man for the good of the Sabbath (Mark 2:27). My paraphrase of that verse would read: "Enjoy the Sabbath! That's what it's for. Stop working, start worshiping, and then . . . enjoy!"

The church in which I grew up placed a long list of restrictions on Sabbath day activities. The restrictions undoubtedly stemmed from a sincere desire to honor God, but I don't think these lists of rigid do's and don'ts were what God had in mind when He gave us this commandment. Rather, I believe that our Sabbath day activities should enhance our physical, emotional, and spiritual recovery in ways that appeal to us personally.

After giving two messages on Sunday morning, I return home exhausted. At that point there's nothing I enjoy more than a simple meal served in the family room, a fat copy of the *Chicago Tribune*, and a televised Chicago Bears football game. With my kids nearby and my wife curled up in an easy chair with a good book, the scene is complete. I usually drift off to sleep during the fourth quarter, and wake up just in time to have a light snack before I greet my weekly discipleship group. For the next two hours we study and memorize Scripture, share personal needs, and pray and laugh and cry together.

By the time I go to bed on Sunday night, I feel as though I've enjoyed a slice of heaven. My body, mind, and spirit are relaxed, and I look forward to the coming week.

Perhaps your idea of a "perfect" Sabbath day differs radically from mine. Maybe you'd prefer to take a walk, ride a bike, play a game, go on a picnic, get together with friends, or any

one of a thousand other things. But whatever we choose to do, it's great to know we have freedom in Christ.

Yes, God wants us to honor the Sabbath by refraining from work, focusing on worship, and engaging in activities that contribute to our physical, emotional, and spiritual renewal. Does that sound like a burdensome command to you?

God asks so little of us, and gives so much in return. Why not honor Him on the Sabbath? Why not adapt your lifestyle to His divinely ordained schedule? You have nothing to lose—and so much to gain!

Week FOUR REFLECTIONS

At the end of this week's readings, take some time to think about how these devotionals have affected you. For example, what spiritual insights have you gained? What practical applications have come to mind? How are your attitudes and/or actions likely to change as a result?

Use your responses as "grist" for your journal and as topics for prayer times with the Lord. In this way, you'll keep a record of your spiritual growth as God works out His will in your life.

For Personal Discovery:

1. Read Mark 2:27 and Hebrews 4:9-11. According to these verses, what is the purpose of Sabbath?

2. Read Genesis 2:1-3, Exodus 23:12, and Isaiah 58:13-14. Based on the teachings of these sample verses, what principles should guide you in determining how to spend your day of rest?

3. It is sometimes easier to maintain material possessions, like cars or houses, than things less measurable, like ourselves or our relationships. How would you rate yourself as to how well you "maintain" yourself? (Consider diet, regular exercise, friendships, etc.) What happens to you when you don't take time to rest on a regular basis?

4. Read Exodus 20:8-11. God elaborates on the fourth commandment because He wants to be perfectly clear about our need for rest. Why do we have to be commanded to rest?

5. How are you making worship with other Christians an integral part of your day of rest? How would you like to improve your personal worship during these times?

Personal Prayer Focus

- Prayerfully meditate on Exodus 20:8-11. Then take time to praise God that He knows we are frail and dependent creatures and has remembered our physical limitations by commanding us to rest on a regular basis and be refreshed by worshiping Him.

- Ask the Holy Spirit to enable you to live a balanced life—one marked by obedience in work as well as rest.

- Examine your own practice of the commandment to take regular rest. Make a list of some specific ways you can make your Sabbath more restful and worshipful. Begin to put these ideas into practice this week. Record in your prayer journal the impact you observe your new choices making on your ability to love God and others.

Journaling My Insights . . .

_____

_____

_____

_____

_____

_____

_____

_____

_____

Fulfill The Cycle Of Love

"Honor your father and your mother, that your days may be prolonged in the land which the Lord your God gives you." Exodus 20:12

This week's devotional theme:

God's commandments include the right ordering of family relationships.

Love God, Love People

Only after thoroughly discussing our relationship with Himself does God move on to the fifth commandment, which addresses our relationships with others. He knows we must be at peace with Him and under the influence of His Spirit before we can hope to relate to others satisfactorily.

Occasionally, non-Christians come to me for counseling because they want to "get their act together" and work on family relationships. They're frustrated because their attempts to be more loving to family members usually end in failure. They can't forgive past wrongs. They can't overlook irritating habits. They can't love someone who seems "unlovable." They don't seem to have it in them. They just can't do it on their own.

I tell such people the same thing I tell myself every day of my life: "Of course you can't do it on your own! You need a love that's not your own—and a patient, forgiving spirit that's not your own. You need a change of heart."

Not long ago a friend of mine had to fire one of his key employees. "Five years ago, before I became a Christian, this would have been easy," he said. "I would have sent the guy a pink slip and said, 'Sorry, you weren't doing the job.' Short, simple, and to the point. This time, however, I agonized over the situation. As soon as I realized this man couldn't handle his responsibilities, I started praying about it. I even tried to alter his job description. But it just didn't work. I knew he had to go. So I flew to the city where his office was located and talked with him personally. I gave him my reasons and promised to help him find another position.

"It was easy to fire people when I didn't care about them. But now that I know the Lord, people and relationships are very important to me. I don't want to use or hurt people, or take their needs lightly. I want to love and encourage them."

That's exactly how every true believer should feel. As we grow in our relationship with God, we should experience a revolutionary change in our attitudes toward people. People should become more important to us. We should become more sensitive to their needs, desires, and hurts.

And guess what: parents are people too!

Children living in the parental home should honor their parents by cooperating with them joyfully, respecting them, and expressing appreciation. Children living outside the family home should make sure their parents' basic needs are met, ought to include them in family activities, and should communicate their love to them over and over again.

Our reward for obeying the fifth commandment will be the blessing of a warm and harmonious family life—and that is a rich blessing indeed. When we're enjoying a right relationship with God and a right relationship with our parents, we have the most important relationships in life in order—and the freedom to establish a right relationship with the world.

First Things First

What relationship has more potential for both love and hate—and joy and sorrow—than the parent-child relationship?

Most experts agree that the family is the birthplace of self-esteem. In the family, children learn their value as human beings. They experiment with their interests, their abilities, and their intellects. They learn to relate to others. And they have the opportunity to see themselves through other people's eyes. As they do these things, they develop a view of themselves—either negative or positive—based on their treatment within the family setting. Have they been accepted, encouraged, and praised? Or have they been ignored, belittled, and criticized? Their self-esteem probably will reflect the answers to those questions.

A properly functioning family is also the birthplace of respect for authority. Children learn in the family that certain lines must be drawn, certain expectations must be met, and certain people must be respected and obeyed. How a child learns about authority in the home will determine how he relates to teachers, coaches, employers, government officials, and ultimately, to God.

Finally, the home is the birthplace of values. By the time a child is a teenager, she knows what's most important to her parents. She knows whether it's success in the marketplace, or pleasure, or money—or if it's relationships and obedience to Jesus Christ. And more likely than not, that teenager will carry those same values into her own adult life.

Obviously, some very important eggs are placed in the family basket. That's why God says so much about the family in Scripture. Many passages in the Psalms, Proverbs, and Epistles admonish parents to create a positive, godly family environment. Other passages, including the fifth commandment, turn the tables and admonish children to do their part in supporting a godly family structure. While parents have a responsibility to be loving, giving, conscientious authority figures, children have a duty to honor their parents in a God-glorifying way.

I suspect that God gave the fifth commandment because He knew how easy it would be for us to develop a disrespectful attitude toward our parents. As children, we're basically selfish; we want everything to go our way. As teenagers, we think our parents are hopelessly ignorant and "behind the times." As young adults, we become consumed with the responsibilities of work and marriage. And, as middle-aged adults, we view the needs of our aged parents as wearisome burdens that infringe on our hard-earned freedom.

This commandment tells us, however, that if we want to have a "right" relationship with God, we have to have a "right" relationship with our parents. We need to honor them the way God tells us to, whether we're younger children still living in our parents' home, or older children living on our own. What's your best evidence to show that you are, indeed, honoring your own parents?

In the Family Home

Imagine a mother, father, and child taking a Sunday afternoon drive through the country. Five-year-old Johnny is standing in the seat between Mom and Dad, and they're all enjoying the fall scenery. As they approach a small town, Dad tells Johnny to sit down and put on his seat belt.

"No way, Dad," Johnny responds with unexpected defiance.

"Maybe you don't understand me, Son," says Dad. "We're coming into heavy traffic and I want you to put your seat belt on."

Again Johnny refuses. "I don't want to, Dad. And I'm not gonna do it."

At this point Mom comes to the rescue and grabs Johnny's little earlobe. As she starts lowering him, she says, "Basically, what your dad means, Johnny, is that you either sit down and buckle up, or you're in big trouble!"

Wisely, Johnny sits down and buckles his seat belt. As he does so, however, he glares at his dad and mumbles, "I might be sitting down on the outside, but I'm standing up on the inside!"

Johnny gave mechanical compliance to his parents' order, but he did so in a state of inner rebellion. That's not what honoring our father and mother is all about.

When Shanna and Todd were little and I would come home from work and find the family room looking like a disaster area, with toys strewn from one end to the other, I would have an impromptu business meeting with my kids. "Todd, Shauna," I would say, "I think we have a little problem here. There's no excuse for a mess like this. I want you to pick up all the toys in this room and put them in the closet—neatly."

At that point, I was not worried about whether the kids would pick up the toys. I knew they would. I was concerned, however, about the attitude with which they would perform this task. Sometimes Todd would pick up a little metal truck, take it over to the closet, and throw it into the box. Crash! Bang! Boom! In the process, he would break two or three little plastic toys—and make it clear that it was time for us to have another little talk.

The Epistle to the Philippians tells us to "do all things without grumbling or disputing" (2:14). Godly obedience is not merely outward acquiescence accompanied by a grudging spirit. When God tells us to obey, He expects us to do it with a spirit of graciousness and cooperation. If you are still living with your parents, please take that verse to heart. Obey God and the fifth commandment by cooperating joyfully with your parents' requests. A grumbling spirit casts a dark shadow over the atmosphere of a home, whereas good-natured obedience is the surest way to ease tension and promote harmony.

Show a Little Appreciation

A great way to honor our parents is by appreciating what they've done for us. Most of us can honestly say that our parents have made a larger investment in our lives than anyone else. I didn't realize that twenty years ago. But the experience of being a parent myself has taught me some valuable lessons.

When my wife became pregnant with our first child, she had no idea what was in store for her. She didn't know she would spend the next nine months fighting desperately to "keep her lunch down." She didn't know that the miraculous, yet traumatic, experience of childbirth would arouse such fears in her. She didn't know that nighttime feedings, dirty diapers, and interrupted plans would be so overwhelming.

Nor did I know how drastically children would alter our lifestyle. Or how hard it would be to coordinate family needs and ministry needs. Or how challenging the role of being a father would be.

It has been estimated that it will cost the average parents hundreds of thousands of dollars to raise one child from infancy to eighteen years of age. But that monetary investment is nothing compared to the investment of time, concern, prayer, and planning that most parents put into their child-rearing practices. My wife and I discussed our children more frequently than any other subject during their formative years. How could we best meet their needs? How could we stimulate their minds? How could we build their self-esteem? How could we help them uncover their strengths and abilities?

Parents have to grapple with these and many other issues. Because we're imperfect, we make mistakes and have regrets. But the fact remains that we make a tremendous investment in the lives of our children. Our love for them demands it.

What's the best way to crush your parents' spirits? Just neglect to show appreciation for what they do. Keep on taking, taking, taking, without ever saying "thank you"—without ever showing gratitude.

On the other hand, what's the best way to lift your parents' spirits? Show a little appreciation. You don't have to get fancy. Just say, "Thanks for preparing that meal. It was great." Or, "I really appreciate the way you do my laundry." Or, "It's nice of you to pick me up from school."

When my kids thank me for simple things, it makes a tremendous difference in my attitude toward parenting. It motivates me to make even greater investments in their lives. The same thing happens when they obey me without an argument or display an attitude of respect. When they honor me, they encourage me to be the best parent I can be.

If your parents are still living, you have hundreds of opportunities every day to offer obedience, respect, and appreciation. Why not take advantage of this? Your parents will benefit by it—and so will you.

Keep On Caring for Them

Some people think the fifth commandment applies only to children living in their parents' home. But I believe it applies across the board. Even if we live outside our parental home and support ourselves—and even if we have families of our own—we are still commanded to honor our parents.

A marvelous cycle is evident in the ongoing life of a family. When a baby is born into a family, he is totally dependent on his parents. As he grows, he becomes increasingly independent, until one day he is ready to leave the home of his youth and establish one of his own. He has followed the God-ordained path to maturity.

His parents, meanwhile, have followed another path designed by God—a path that has taken them from the vitality of youth and the security of middle age to the vulnerability of old age. In that final state, they become dependent on the children they have raised, and the cycle is complete.

I've personally seen this cycle illustrated at its best in my wife's family. For years, Lynne's mother provided at-home care for her own invalid mother. Lynne and I often made special plans with Lynne's parents, only to have them interrupted by Grandma's needs. And repeatedly over the years, Lynne's father had to alter his lifestyle to make room for his aged mother-in-law.

Compared to the treatment most elderly parents receive in this society, Lynne's grandmother was treated wonderfully. But it's even more amazing when you realize that her family helped her without the slightest hint of complaint or resentment. While Lynne and her brother were growing up, they considered it a privilege to have Grandma with them all the time. They thought they were the luckiest kids in the neighborhood. They cherished the special relationship they enjoyed with her. Lynne's mother thought it was only natural to provide a warm and loving home for the woman who had done the same for her many years earlier. What a testimony of love this has been to me!

I see this kind of loving concern illustrated in the life of Jesus too. Even during His time of greatest need, our Lord turned His attention toward His mother. Imagine Him on the cross, hanging naked between heaven and earth with the weight of our sin on His shoulders. For an instant, Jesus opens His eyes and sees His mother. He knows how much she'll miss the support of her eldest son, so He asks John to care for her— as a mother. John obviously knew what his master meant, for Scripture tells us that "from that hour the disciple took her into his own household" (John 19:27).

Often, our excuse for not caring for our parents is that we don't have time. But even Jesus took time to make sure His mother was properly cared for, and we should do no less.

Week FIVE REFLECTIONS

At the end of this week's readings, take some time to think about how these devotionals have affected you. For example, what spiritual insights have you gained? What practical applications have come to mind? How are your attitudes and/or actions likely to change as a result?

Use your responses as "grist" for your journal and as topics for prayer times with the Lord. In this way, you'll keep a record of your spiritual growth as God works out His will in your life.

For Personal Discovery:

1. How did your mother and father demonstrate (either positively or negatively) the value of "honor" to each other? How has their example impacted your understanding of the concept?

2. Read Exodus 20:12. What do you think it means to "honor" your parents? Why do you think this commandment is placed at the beginning of the commands concerning our relationships with others?

3. Read Matthew 15:3-9. Jesus makes it clear that true love for God is demonstrated by how we treat others—in this case, our parents. What was wrong with the way the Pharisees observed the fifth commandment? What are some ways that we, too, might dishonor our parents?

4. Some people think that this commandment requires children (no matter how old) to do whatever their parents say. What do you think? Is honoring the same as obeying? Explain.

5. If one or both of your parents are not believers, how can you better demonstrate Christian love for them through your words and actions?

Personal Prayer Focus

- Pray for your parents' spiritual and physical well-being.

- Confess (without making excuses for) any negligent behavior or thoughts on your part in obeying God's command to honor your parents.

- Ask the Holy Spirit for wisdom and sensitivity to know how to honor your parents more fully and genuinely. For example: Make a list of things you can do to show your parents honor in ways that are meaningful to them. These can be one-time acts or ongoing items. Determine to fulfill several items on your list during the course of the next few months.

Journaling My Insights . . .

_____

_____

_____

_____

_____

_____

_____

_____

_____

_____

_____

Destroy The Killer In You

"You shall not murder." Exodus 20:13

This week's devotional theme:

The sixth commandment speaks to the root of
the spirit of violence and all its manifestations.

We Have No Right

I remember the first time I heard the term, "Chicago-style murder." While reading an East Coast newspaper, I came across headlines announcing a gruesome gangland slaying. A subtitle called the murder a "Chicago-style hit."

The beautiful city on the lake first earned this aspect of its reputation during the Al Capone era of the '20s and '30s. But a wide variety of underground figures have conscientiously perpetuated it. Chicago is still one of the "contract capitals" of the world, and its citizens continue to make national headlines by inflicting multiple gunshot wounds on one another, hiding dead bodies in car trunks, and using "cement slippers" to assure former friends a place at the bottom of the Chicago River.

But we all know that it's not fair to pick solely on Chicago. Chicago-style murders are nothing new, and they're certainly not confined to the Windy City. Throughout history, men and women have been wielding rocks, knives, axes, swords, and spears against their neighbors. Whether they've been motivated by anger, hatred, greed, fear, or jealousy, the outcome often has been the same—murder.

The first biblically recorded homicide is described in Genesis 4. In a fit of jealousy and anger, Adam's firstborn son, Cain, slew his brother, Abel. Imagine the horror of the scene. No living being had ever witnessed the awful spectacle of human death. Yet there before Adam and Eve lay the cold, lifeless body of their son—flesh of their flesh and bone of their bone.

Imagine the questions that raced through their minds. *Cain, how could you? How dare you? What right did you have to decide that Abel should die? You're not God!*

Such questions reveal the heinous nature of murder. God creates and sustains men and women, and He alone has the right to number their days. When humans pirate God's prerogative to control life and death, they commit an unspeakable offense before God, the victim, and society. The sixth commandment says no one but God has the right to determine when a person should die.

Surely, this law also applies to suicide and abortion, as well as to willful acts of violence that stop short of death. At this point in history, child abuse has become a national nightmare, and battered wives keep hotlines busy and shelters full. Statistics tell us that unprecedented numbers of Americans live in private torture chambers, where violence is passed from one generation to the next. Can we doubt the need for a prohibition against violence? How will you, personally, contribute to its demise in the year ahead?

Different Folks, Different Styles

Even professional athletes often use unnecessary violence. It's pretty hard to justify the fighter who turns his opponent's face into a bloody mask, and then says jubilantly, "I just wanted to pound his head in!" But we don't even let it bother us. Similarly, we leave hockey games disappointed if we don't see a brawl, and we closely watch the late-night news to see recaps of the day's sporting violence.

After the news, we let the late-night movie chill us with true-to-life horror stories. And we corporately pour billions of dollars into a film industry that turns violence into entertainment.

All the while, God points to the sixth commandment and says, "Don't you understand? I have a better plan. I don't want men to sleep with pistols under their pillows. I don't want women to carry mace in their purses. I don't want every door in every house to be triple-locked. My people shouldn't have to live that way. So don't kill each other. Don't abuse one another. And don't condone violence. Please, please, please—obey the sixth commandment!"

More Than One Way to Murder

At first glance, the sixth commandment appears to be the easiest of the ten to obey. Most of us have never killed anyone and certainly don't intend to. So why waste time addressing this issue? Why not move on to commandment number seven?

Well, before we decide we're free to bypass this commandment, perhaps we should hear what Jesus had to say about it:

"You have heard that the ancients were told, 'You shall not commit murder' and 'Whoever commits murder shall be liable to the court.' But I say to you that everyone who is angry with his brother shall be guilty before the court; and whoever shall say to his brother, 'Raca,' shall be guilty before the supreme court; and whoever shall say, 'You fool,' shall be guilty enough to go into the hell of fire" (Matt. 5:21-22).

In simple terms, Jesus was telling us there's more than one way to murder a person. And I think He'd say the same thing today. He'd tell those of us who live in nice neighborhoods, who work for nice companies, and who attend nice churches, that there are murderers in our midst. Oh, they may not be Chicago-style murderers, but they are killers, nonetheless.

All from the Same Source

Most people who read this book are far too civilized and controlled to participate in the kinds of Chicago-style slayings I spoke of in Day One. Sophisticated suburbanites that we are, we use our guns for show or target practice. We use our knives to cut our gourmet quiche. The only slippers we're familiar with are the ones we step into en route to our easy chairs.

Oh yes, we're a far different breed from the Chicago-style killers. But I wouldn't be surprised if we're exactly the kind of people Jesus spoke to in Matthew 5:21-22. We wouldn't think of lifting a gun or a knife against another person, but we destroy them just the same. We harbor unresolved anger that displays itself in a hateful attitude toward others. Or, like Jesus' contemporaries, we question other men's worth by calling them *raca*—good for nothing. And what does Jesus say about people who do these things? That they are worthy of hell—just like murderers.

In His words in Matthew, Jesus reveals the striking similarity between physical and verbal violence. There is little difference between a dripping knife and juicy gossip, between racing bullets and an abusive tongue. Why? Because they all flow from the same source—a hateful heart. And they all kill.

I recognize such tendencies in my own heart, especially when it comes to looking down on others and committing verbal violence with the thoughts of my heart. Over and over again I've had to confess the hardness of my heart and admit that I'm a pious killer. No swords. No slander. But so often, no mercy either.

When I started working on this week of devotionals, I thought this commandment about murder was going to be a breeze. As it turned out, this has been the most personally challenging section for me so far. I've been forced to admit that far too often I slip into the role of a killer. How I pray that God will transform me daily, and change the hatred in my heart to love, the violence to tenderness, the slander to encouragement, the apathy to a God-inspired activism.

Are you willing to let God destroy the killer in you? Do you dare yield your heart to His transforming power? Will you commit yourself to using your hands for tenderness, your words for encouragement, and your resources for the good of the needy? Will you?

Are You a Suburban-Style Killer?

When Chicago-style murderers kill, they usurp God's right to number a man's days. When suburban-style murderers kill, they usurp God's right to measure a man's worth.

Man, created in God's image, is the crown of all Creation. He is God's masterpiece, His most priceless possession. As such, he has great value—not, of course, because he deserves it—but because God chooses to value him. That is an indisputable and blessed biblical truth. God deems man valuable, precious, worthy.

Who are we, then, to decide that some men and women are not worthy, or precious, or valuable? Who are we to decide that they can be called a loser, or fool, or redneck, or spick, or Chink? What right do we have to crush their spirits by insulting them, humiliating them, or discriminating against them? We have no right to do those things—absolutely none!

Before I started working on this section, I assumed that I'd be able to stand guiltless before the sixth commandment. I now realize that all too often I've adopted the role of the suburban-style murderer. With careless insensitivity, and sometimes even malice, I've ripped people to shreds with my words. And I stand before God guilty, desperately needing His forgiveness.

Do you, too, need to confess the sin of murder? If we're serious about honoring God, we must be serious about dealing with the sixth commandment. James tells us that with the same tongue we "bless our Lord and Father; and with it we curse men, who have been made in the likeness of God; from the same mouth come both blessing and cursing. My brethren, these things ought not to be this way" (3:9-10). We can't use our mouths to worship God one minute, and then use them to abuse people the next.

Perhaps we need to look back in history to a bloodstained cross. Perhaps we need to look again at a dying Savior who had every right to curse us for violating His Father's holiness with our sin. Yes, He had the right to do that. But what did He do instead? He looked at us through the eyes of unfathomable love, took our sins on Himself, and freed us from the doom of eternal death.

Jesus wasn't forced to do that. He chose to do it because He loved us. And now He wants to pour that same love into our hearts so we can show it to others. King David earnestly begged God to create in him a clean heart and to renew his spirit (Ps. 51:10). We have to do that as well. We need to ask God to replace the hatred in our hearts with love, the arrogance with humility, the bitterness with tolerance, and the malice with understanding. We need a nonviolent heart so we can speak nonviolent words.

O Father, forgive us for being suburban-style killers. Purify us so we can obey Your command.

Religious-style Murderers

Chicago-style killers are a brash bunch. Their crimes are grue-some, easy to detect, and deadly. Suburban-style killers are more subtle, and their crimes less visible; but their attacks are just as direct—and just as deadly. There's a third type of killer, however, whose methods differ drastically from the others'. These killers commit no murderous acts and use neither their hands nor their tongues. They kill simply by neglect and apa-thy. They kill by withholding that which sustains life—love and attention.

Of course, these people would never call themselves killers. But that's exactly what they are—pious, self-righteous, religious-style killers. And Jesus condemned them to the fate all unrepentant murderers deserve. Why? The reason is found in Christ's own words:

"I was hungry, and you gave Me nothing to eat; I was thirsty, and you gave Me nothing to drink; I was a stranger, and you did not invite Me in; naked, and you did not clothe Me; sick, and in prison, and you did not visit Me" (Matt. 25:42-43).

"I know you didn't plunge a sword into My side, as a Chicago-style killer would have done," Jesus is saying. "And I know you didn't make fun of Me, as a suburban-style killer would have. But you gave Me no food when I was hungry. You gave Me no coat when I was cold. So I died. There was no sword, no slander—but no help either. And now My blood is on your hands."

Our church periodically sponsors food drives. On a given Sunday morning, church members bring in bags of groceries that are used to stock the shelves of our church-operated Food Pantry. The Pantry then distributes the food to needy families in our church and community. Another portion of the food is distributed to disadvantaged families in the inner city.

Most people in our church wholeheartedly support this program. In fact, they look forward to expanding this particular ministry. But I know that each time I announce a food drive, a few individuals think, *Oh boy, here we go again—another handout request. Why do they keep begging me for help? I work hard. I pay my bills. I take care of my family. Let those other people do the same. They're not my responsibility.*

If you find yourself echoing those words, maybe you need to take another look at a dying Savior. Maybe you need a new heart. I'm well acquainted with our natural tendency to isolate ourselves in our own little worlds and ignore the needy. How easy it is for me to say, "Hey, I've got my loving wife, my precious kids, my sport utility vehicle, and my cozy home in the suburbs. This is my world. If people outside it are hungry and naked and dying—well, I hope somebody takes care of them."

Do you hear the murder in words like those?

At the end of this week's readings, take some time to think about how these devotionals have affected you. For example, what spiritual insights have you gained? What practical applications have come to mind? How are your attitudes and/or actions likely to change as a result?

Use your responses as "grist" for your journal and as topics for prayer times with the Lord. In this way, you'll keep a record of your spiritual growth as God works out His will in your life.

For Personal Discovery:

1. Read Exodus 20:13 and Matthew 5:21-22. Why does Jesus make a parallel between physical violence and verbal violence? What does He say will be the fate of both?

2. Besides cold-blooded killing, what other acts of violence are probably included in the prohibition against "murder"?

3. What actually is "killed" when you misuse the weapon of your mouth? Why is this kind of murder just as heinous in God's eyes as actually killing someone with a knife or a gun?

4. Read James 3:9-12. What is James saying about the one who professes to love God, yet does not love people who are made in God's image?

5. We've discussed "Chicago-style" murder, "suburban-style" murder, and "religious-style" murder. What is meant by each? In what ways is each of these "murders" a violation of the sixth command?

6. Read Matthew 25:31-46. Why do we often resent our responsibility to care for the needy?

Personal Prayer Focus

• Read aloud the prayer of St. Francis:

> Lord,
> Make me an instrument of Your peace.
> Where there is hatred, let me sow love;
> where there is injury, pardon;
> where there is doubt, faith;
> where there is despair, hope;
> where there is darkness, light;
> where there is sadness, joy.

• Ask the Holy Spirit, who dwells in you and empowers you to obey God's commands, to make you sensitive to the power of your words.

Journaling My Insights . . .

_____

_____

_____

_____

_____

_____

_____

_____

_____

Week
SEVEN

Keep Pleasure
Undefiled

"You shall not commit adultery."
Exodus 20:14

This week's devotional theme:
God wants to safeguard the sanctity
of sex within marriage.

Even If You've Already Slipped . . .

"Hey, Adam," God says. "I have a little surprise for you. I've been waiting for just the right time, and I think this is it. You take a little nap, and when you wake up, you're going to have a real treat waiting for you!"

While Adam sleeps, God takes one of his ribs and fashions it into a woman; He then breathes into her nostrils the breath of life. When Adam wakes, she's waiting for him—living, breathing, shapely, long-haired Eve.

What do you think Adam did at that point? The Bible only tells us that he called her "bone of my bones, and flesh of my flesh" (Gen. 2:23), but I think that simple statement reveals the depth of his identification with her. Here at last was one who was like him, someone with whom he could share all things, with whom he could commune at the deepest level. Good-bye loneliness; hello love!

God revealed His view of Adam and Eve's special companionship when He said, "For this cause a man shall leave his father and his mother, and shall cleave to his wife; and they shall become one flesh" (Gen. 2:24). This man and woman were to have a unique relationship, a relationship in which they would be joined together in the flesh, beautifully and intimately, in a way ordained by God.

Now you may be starting to get sweaty palms and a churning stomach as I get deeper into this subject of marriage and the faithful commitment it requires. Why? Because in your mind you may carry the unburied memory of your own adulterous sin. If that describes you, please read these next words carefully. God's grace is bigger than your sin. Jesus' blood can cleanse you and He is willing to forgive you.

I want to start out with this kind of affirmation right at the start, because there is no reason for you to carry a burden of guilt for adultery committed in the past. Right now you can confess your sin to God and claim His forgiveness. God always offers mercy to a repentant sinner. When Jesus met the woman caught in adultery, He didn't condemn her. He sensed her repentant spirit and said, "Go your way; from now on sin no more" (John 8:11).

That's the same thing He's saying to you. So confess your sin, ask God's forgiveness, and then commit yourself to faithfulness in your marriage.

I can't guarantee that your spouse will have the same forgiving spirit God has. I can say, however, that I've had the pleasure of seeing more than one violated partner forgive a repentant spouse. I have witnessed firsthand the complete rebuilding of a destroyed marriage, as both husband and wife committed themselves to restoring a foundation of trust and respect and loyalty. This didn't happen overnight. And it could never have occurred without the intervention of God's healing Spirit. But it did happen. And it can happen to other people who are willing to repent and forgive.

You've Got to Be Kidding!

Some people are shocked to learn that God is "pro-sex." Having heard so many erroneous analyses of God's view of sex, they find it hard to accept the truth—that the holy God of Israel, the author of the Ten Commandments, is the foremost proponent of healthy sex.

Yet Scripture clearly reveals this fact. We learn from the Creation account that the sexual dimension of our personality is woven into the very fabric of who we are as human beings. Physiologically and psychologically, we are created to be sexual beings. The physical attraction between male and female was no accident, and it certainly was not the result of evil. It was a beautiful and important part of God's wise design.

Furthermore, Scripture seems to indicate that God created human sexuality primarily for pleasure. Procreation appears to be a secondary purpose. God first spoke of man and woman "becoming one flesh" within the context of ending Adam's isolation and loneliness (Gen. 2:18-25); the role of procreation is not mentioned until later.

We see a "pro-sex" attitude not only in Genesis, but in the rest of the Bible as well. The Song of Solomon is a poetic description of the romantic and erotic attraction between two lovers. Many commentators view it as a reflection of what Adam may have felt when God provided Eve as his wife.

The Apostle Paul also tells married couples not to deprive one another of sex, but to engage in it regularly. This rule, he says, has only one exception: By mutual agreement, a couple may abstain from sex for a brief period of time while they devote themselves more fully to prayer (1 Cor. 7:5).

We know that God is "pro-sex." We know that Scripture is "pro-sex." Now, doesn't it follow that Christians should be "pro-sex"? Why should we deny a God-designed dimension of our human makeup?

How tragic that a dark shadow can be cast over a dimension of life that God designed to be beautiful. But, while tragic, it really should come as no surprise; we seem to be masters at shading and distorting the beautiful things God has created. In fact, it appears that anything God can create, man can pervert.

That is precisely why God gave us the seventh commandment. He wanted to make sure sex always would be a tool for unity, not for division. He wanted to keep it beautiful by keeping it pure and undefiled. The seventh commandment is not my law, nor is it merely a human opinion sanctioned by church tradition. It is God's direct provision for protecting His creation.

The Marriage Bed Defiled

I know, sex is a risky business. That's why God confines it to marriage, where a covenant has been made, where a lifelong commitment has been promised. In that environment, trust and security can grow, and gradually fear, anxiety, and inhibition can subside. For sex to be all God intended it to be, it must occur in a marriage relationship based on solid communication patterns, mutual devotion, respect, confidentiality, and above all, absolute loyalty. Only in that kind of relational environment can we expect to have a truly satisfying sexual experience.

My wife and I have found that our level of sexual enjoyment always is proportionate to the overall quality of our marriage. Sex counselors too affirm that basic truth. The sexual dimension of marriage often can be viewed as a barometer of the level of tension or harmony that exists in other areas of the marriage. A poor physical relationship may indicate broken communication patterns or a lack of devotion, respect, and trust. A healthy physical relationship probably indicates open communication lines and a high degree of warmth, loyalty, and mutual support. Sex is so much more than just physical intercourse. It is a God-ordained means of communicating love, a mutually enjoyable means of sealing a commitment, and the ultimate expression of vulnerability and trust.

Against that backdrop, we can see why adultery is such a serious offense. A person who commits this sin is not just violating an oath. He is violating another person. It is not the adulterous sexual relationship, itself, that is so destructive; it is the accompanying deceit, dishonesty, and disloyalty that shatter marriages and threaten the self-esteem of the violated partner.

"How could you deceive me like this?" a husband or wife asks. "How could you lie and mock my trust?"

That's where the agony comes in. And it's an agony that's almost unbearable. I had been in the ministry for only two years when I had to sit down with a young father and help him tell his two little children that Mommy wasn't coming home anymore; she had moved away with another man. The pain of that experience burned its way into my mind so deeply that I hoped never to get involved in another situation like that again. But I have gotten involved. Why? Because over the years men and women have continued to violate their spouses. And violated, broken spouses have continued to knock on the door to my office.

Hollywood makes the free and easy lifestyle of adultery appear so glamorous. But it's a blatant lie. Adultery causes pain. Everybody loses. Everybody suffers. Everybody is scarred. If adultery leads to divorce, as it so often does, the pain can last a lifetime.

God wants to spare us this pain. He wants to protect us, our spouses, and our families. He wants our marriages to be pure and undefiled, havens of love, trust, warmth, and pleasure. He wants sex to be a tool for building unity into our marriages—not a weapon for destroying them. Please don't toy with the seventh commandment.

The Popular Sin

Some people assume that the only sexual prohibition in the Bible is the one against adultery. They believe unmarried people can legitimately engage in sexual activities as long as their partner also is not married. I hate to rain on their parade, but I have to tell them that they're categorically wrong. Obviously, they haven't worn out their Bibles looking for instruction on sexual relationships!

The biblical term for premarital sex—any sex engaged in by unmarried persons—is fornication, and Scripture explicitly prohibits it. Matthew lists fornication right after murder and adultery (15:19), and Ephesians tells us that sexual immorality shouldn't even be mentioned as an option among Christians (5:3). It should be the farthest thing from our minds. Sex belongs in marriage, and only in marriage.

Remember, God wants sexual activity to be enjoyed within the context of a secure, permanent relationship. Bed-hopping is a gross distortion of God's plan. It strips the sexual relationship of the one-to-one intimacy that makes it special and valuable. It separates sex from the loving commitment that gives it meaning.

But some people will say, "You don't understand. We're not bed-hopping. We're not running from partner to partner. We're not buying sex. We're in love and we plan to be married someday. Why shouldn't we enjoy sex now?"

My response is that it's true that sex is not dirty, ugly, or evil. It's beautiful, pure, and holy—but only when it's enjoyed by people who love God and are willing to obey the guidelines He has established. Some time ago, a couple with no previous church background visited our worship service. My message that day was a simple explanation of the Gospel, and apparently, its basic truths made sense to this couple. Within weeks, both had accepted Christ as their Savior. They then came to my office to ask a few questions and to get some reading material. During the course of our conversation, I learned that they had been living together for seven years, unmarried, in a home they had purchased jointly.

Their hearts sank when I told them their living arrangement was not pleasing to God. If they really meant business with God, they would have to make a change.

The woman acknowledged that the Lord meant more to her than her living arrangements, and decided to move out. Her boyfriend agreed with her decision and made arrangements for her to move in with his parents. They then established a pattern of sexual purity which they maintained until their marriage almost a year later.

They've been married several years now, and it's obvious God's hand is on them. They readily admit that the turning point in their relationship and in their spiritual lives was the day they decided to become sexually pure. I challenge those of you who are living in sexual sin to follow their example.

It Starts in the Heart

Jesus said, "You have heard that it was said, 'You shall not commit adultery'; but I say to you, that everyone who looks on a woman to lust for her has committed adultery with her already in his heart" (Matt. 5:27-28).

In this message to the multitude, Jesus did what He had done so many times before. He looked behind an outward expression of sin and saw its inner manifestation. While the outward expression of sexual impurity is adultery or fornication, the inner manifestation is lust. To many people, lust seems innocent—or if not quite innocent, at least not worth mentioning. After all, they say, its only playground is the mind. But what happens in the mind is important—very important—for it is in the mind that the battle for sexual purity must be fought.

All of us notice attractive members of the opposite sex now and then. Attraction and stimulation are normal reactions for sexual beings, such as we are. Obviously, that normal reaction does not constitute the lust to which Jesus referred in Matthew 5.

No, it's not the first, casual look that constitutes lust. Nor is it the innocent appreciation of a muscular physique, a shapely body, or a pretty face. It's the second, third, or fourth look—the look that's accompanied by an imagined seduction, a mental undressing, and a conscious fantasy of having a sexual relationship with that person—that defines lust. That is what Jesus forbade.

A mind that persistently dreams and schemes and seduces is a mind that needs cleansing. Jesus calls lust "adultery in the heart," and like any other sexual sin, it must be confessed and abandoned. If we don't confess and turn away from it, it eventually will consume our thoughts. And if we encourage it with sexually stimulating films, books, magazines, or social settings, we'll probably yield to the temptation—and turn the fantasy into reality.

Please don't do that. Don't fill your mind with garbage. When we flirt with sin, we eventually fall prey to it—and then we have to pay the price of disobedience.

God loves us and wants to liberate us. That's why He gave us the seventh commandment. He wants to free our minds from the shadow of sin so that we can think constructively, worship joyfully, and relate to other people in pure and healthy ways. He doesn't want to deny us the pleasures of life. He simply wants to keep our pleasures undefiled.

At the end of this week's readings, take some time to think about how these devotionals have affected you. For example, what spiritual insights have you gained? What practical applications have come to mind? How are your attitudes and/or actions likely to change as a result?

Use your responses as "grist" for your journal and as topics for prayer times with the Lord. In this way, you'll keep a record of your spiritual growth as God works out His will in your life.

For Personal Discovery:

1. Think about the last movie you saw. What perspective toward sex did that movie promote? Then read Exodus 20:14 and Matthew 5:27-30. Come up with your working definition of "adultery."

2. Sometimes it's easier to try to reason a way out of following God's will (Adam blamed Eve for his disobedience and Eve blamed the serpent for hers). List some ways we try to excuse wrong thinking and behavior instead of taking personal responsibility.

3. Since God has designed sex to be an expression of love, why is it not okay to have sex with someone you really love prior to marriage?

4. What hope and help would you offer a Christian who felt guilt about past sexual sins?

5. If you are married, what are some specific ways you can affirm your commitment to be faithful to your spouse? If you are not currently married, what are some specific ways you can affirm your commitment to be faithful to the Lord as well as to a possible future spouse?

Personal Prayer Focus

- Prayerfully read John 14:15. Ask the Lord to forgive you for dwelling on impure thoughts or behaving in an "adulterous" manner. Confess your need for God's grace and mercy as you commit to follow His commands.

- Express your thanks to Christ for His death on the cross, which makes it possible for you to experience forgiveness for your sins and to live a life with God instead of apart from Him.

- Reflect on the perspective toward sexuality that you were raised with. Was the attitude permissive, repressive, or relatively balanced? Think about some of the reasons behind this perspective. Record your insights in the journaling section below.

If you are married, ask yourself: "What am I doing now to establish a lifetime of sexual pleasure with my spouse alone?" Create an opportunity to communicate with your spouse how you can better satisfy each other's sexual interests.

Journaling My Insights . . .

_____

_____

_____

_____

_____

_____

_____

Acquire By The Rules

"You shall not steal." Exodus 20:15

This week's devotional theme:

God entrusts us with personal property acquired
through work and gifts; stealing violates that trust.

Day ONE

The Wrong Way to Get It

It was Christmas Eve. My sister Ginny was driving home from a late-night service at her church. The trees lining the country road glistened momentarily as they caught the beam of her headlights. The wet snow gathered in icy mounds on her windshield wipers and left a thin layer of slippery moisture on the narrow road. As Ginny slowly rounded a sloping curve, she noticed a car stuck in a snowdrift at the bottom of the hill.

Dismissing the recollected warnings that floated through her mind about stopping to help strangers, she pulled her car off the road and offered assistance.

"I can't believe you stopped," said the man in the car. "I was afraid I'd be stuck here all night. Maybe if you drive the car while I push it, we can get it out."

The two of them worked at it for nearly forty-five minutes, and sure enough, they managed to get the car out of the drift. Ginny drove it to the top of the hill, then ran back down to get her own car.

"Thank you very much," the anonymous stranger said. "You've been a tremendous help to me." He then reached into her car, grabbed her purse—filled with money and credit cards—and said, "Thanks again. This will do nicely." He ran up the hill, got into his car, and drove away.

Ginny watched in disbelief.

Violated!

If you've ever had anything stolen from you, you know the sudden feelings of frustration and violation which accompany that experience. *How could someone do this to me?* you ask. *What did I do to deserve it? Why me? What audacity!*

Whenever something is stolen or taken from us—whether it's hard-earned money, an irreplaceable keepsake, or an expensive necessity—we feel angry and offended. It's not because we worship what we own, or because we equate our worth with our possessions. It's simply that we have a deep-seated need to protect our personal property rights. We believe that if we agree to leave another person's possessions alone, he should agree to respect our property as well. If he violates that assumed agreement, we feel offended.

And so does God. Despite the ongoing political debate over whether private citizens should own personal property, the Bible apparently assumes that individuals will own a certain amount of their own property. The eighth commandment protects such holdings by absolutely forbidding stealing—which is the illegitimate acquisition of property. Be careful that all you obtain is gotten by honorable means.

Shades of Seizure

Many of us respond to God's prohibition against stealing in the same way we react to His prohibition against murder: Why waste time on this commandment? I'm no thief. I would never seize another person's possessions. Let's move on.

But I think I can safely say that just as it's possible to murder a man in more than one fashion, it's also possible to steal from him in a variety of ways. There are shades of seizure that seem almost innocent on the surface, but in reality, they fit squarely within the context of theft.

What about employees helping themselves to company supplies without permission—automotive parts, tools, staplers, paper, pencils, pens, notebooks, computer disks, food? Just take a little here and there. It's no big deal. Or is it? Is helping yourself to another person's property a biblical means of acquiring property? You didn't labor for it. You didn't invest, barter, or trade for it. You didn't pray for it. You didn't even ask for it. The fact is, you stole it.

Several retailers I know have said they lose more merchandise through employee theft than through public theft. They fear their allies more than their enemies. They're more paranoid about being ripped off from the inside than from the outside. What does that tell us? It indicates that people are getting very comfortable with the practice of helping themselves to what is not rightfully theirs.

Another shade of seizure is long-term borrowing. What about the neighbor's ladder you borrowed two years ago? Or that paintbrush or punch bowl or serving platter? How about those books, tapes, and CDs? You said you'd return them, but did you? Did you truly borrow them? Or did you quietly claim them as yours simply by neglecting to return them?

I challenge you, as I've had to challenge myself, to take out a pencil and paper and make a list of everything in your possession that is not rightfully yours. List everything you've taken from your place of employment, everything you've "borrowed" from the shop, everything you've received on loan from friends and neighbors. Then, make a covenant between yourself and God to return everything on your list to its proper owner by the end of the month.

Maybe you'll have to pack some things up in a UPS box and send them back to their owner. Perhaps you'll have to send a money order to cover the cost of supplies and articles you've already used, lost, or broken. You might want to include a note explaining that you now realize what you did was wrong. You've decided to honor God and cleanse your conscience by admitting your sin and making restitution.

You could sign your note, "A Convicted Christian," but I think "A Liberated Christian" might be more accurate. Stealing jeopardizes our self-esteem, produces anxiety, and destroys our credibility as Christians. But repentance and restitution free us. They release us from the binding chains of guilt, and allow us to establish peace with ourselves, with others, and with God.

A Serious Warning!

The problem of stealing has a flip side that may hit more of us where we live: it's the longing for security that accompanies our desire to keep acquiring more and more. But will we ever have enough? I once heard a speaker remark that he never saw a hearse pulling a U-Haul. Though said in jest, that simple saying holds a wealth of truth.

Jesus expressed the same thought when He shared the parable of the rich man who tore down his barns and built bigger ones to contain all his wealth. The man viewed his vast treasure and said to himself, "Take your ease, eat, drink and be merry." But God said to him, "You fool! This very night your soul is required of you; and now who will own what you have prepared?" (Luke 12:16-21) Said Jesus, "So is the man who lays up treasure for himself, and is not rich toward God."

In childhood Sunday School classes, we learn that it is more important to build up treasure in heaven than to amass treasure on earth. But how do we do that? How can we be "rich toward God"? Scripture makes it clear that we store up treasures in heaven each time we use the resources God has given us to accomplish His will in the world. Each time we allow our resources to spill over into other people's lives—when we give to the needy, or support the ministry of the church—we build our account in heaven.

Many men and women have become so caught up in the business of "wheeling and dealing" that they've neglected the most important issues of life. Like the rich man in Jesus' parable, their barns overflow, but their souls are empty. Are you one of those people? If you had to strip away the armor of your wealth, who would you be? If you had to stand before God

Seizure and deception are very similar in the eyes of God. They're both forms of stealing. That's why we need to be careful about how we present our information, our products, and our services.

Paul tells us to speak "the truth in love" (Eph. 4:15). That means that sometimes the Realtor may have to say, "This is a nice house, and I could see you living in it. But I know your financial condition, and I'm afraid the payments would put you under." The produce salesman would have to say, "I have 500 cases of lettuce, but I'm not sure it's as fresh as you'd like it. Why don't you check through a few cases, see how it looks, and we'll strike a deal." The repairman might have to say, "I don't think you really need a new furnace. You could get by with your present one for a few more years."

We may be able to deceive other people, but we can never deceive God. He won't be mocked. He won't be taken in by our clever schemes. What we sow, we will also reap. If we sow dishonesty, we will reap condemnation. But if we sow honesty, integrity, and concern for others, we will reap God's blessing.

Defrauding: It's Stealing Too

Several years ago, my mother loaned $1,000 to a man who had been a friend of my father's. He signed a promissory note, agreeing to repay the money in six months. Six months passed, with no repayment and no request for an extension. Then one year passed, then eighteen months, then two years. She decided to remain patient.

Not long thereafter, my mother went out for dinner with some of her friends. As she arrived at the restaurant, she saw this man drive up in a brand-new car. He got out, said "Hi" to my mother, and walked into the restaurant.

Mom called me the next day and firmly suggested that I confront the man. "Doesn't the Bible say something about his behavior?" she asked.

Yes, the Bible does say something about that. It calls this type of activity defrauding, and forbids it. When we use our creditors' money for unnecessary goods and services, we are defrauding them by withholding that which is rightfully theirs.

Actually, many ways exist to defraud people. One method was used in our church parking lot not long ago. A man who had just started attending our church ordered a new car for his wife, but before the car arrived, he was killed in a tragic airplane accident. His widow continued coming to church and showed Lynne and me her new car as soon as it arrived. Naturally, she had strong sentimental ties to the car because it was the last gift her husband had given her.

During one of our church services, someone ran into her new car and did several hundred dollars' worth of damage. Naturally, the widow was grieved by the damage done to it, but she was even more hurt by the fact that the person who hit her car failed to acknowledge it. He or she left no explanatory note, no notice to the church office, and no offer to cover expenses.

The man or woman who hit that car is guilty of stealing $300 from a young widow. And in the process, he or she damaged the witness of our church, left our elders with a sticky problem to solve, and laid one more weight on the shoulders of a woman who already was immensely burdened.

Unfortunately, such duplicitous behavior is not unique. It's become quite fashionable to defraud the government by failing to declare certain income, or by taking questionable deductions. It's also a common practice to defraud the company by calling in sick when we're not, by making personal phone calls when they're forbidden, or by padding expense accounts when we're traveling. Many people even defraud their families by withholding alimony or child support. But these practices, though common, are not acceptable. We have no right to defraud anyone else—whether that means a young widow, a friend or relative, a credit officer, our company, the government . . . or God.

At the end of this week's readings, take some time to think about how these devotionals have affected you. For example, what spiritual insights have you gained? What practical applications have come to mind? How are your attitudes and/or actions likely to change as a result?

Use your responses as "grist" for your journal and as topics for prayer times with the Lord. In this way, you'll keep a record of your spiritual growth as God works out His will in your life.

For Personal Discovery:

1. When were you tempted to take something that wasn't yours, but chose not to (this could be something tangible, like a basketball, or intangible, like an idea). Why did you choose not to steal?

2. Proverbs 20:23 says God detests "differing weights." In what two or three ways could you conduct your business or personal relationships more equitably?

3. The Bible teaches that certain means of acquiring are acceptable: diligent labor (Eph. 4:28), investment (Matt. 25:14-30), and faithful prayer (Matt. 7:7-11). What makes these means legitimate?

4. Do you think that it is all right to enjoy the possessions you gain through hard work or as a gift? Explain your answer.

5. Read Matthew 6:19-20 and Luke 12:16-21. We store up "treasures in heaven" each time we use the resources God has given us to accomplish His will in the world. What are some specific ways you can be "rich toward God" and thereby build up treasures in heaven?

Personal Prayer Focus

- Read aloud Matthew 16:26 and take a minute to meditate on its meaning.

- Confess your sin to God. Ask Him to strengthen you to obey His commandment not to steal in all its various forms.

- Make a list of everything you have "borrowed" from someone and promised to return but haven't (the neighbor's wheelbarrow, office supplies from work, etc.). Then make a covenant between yourself and God to return everything on your list to its proper owner by the end of the month.

- Meditate this week on Psalm 24:1, James 1:17, and Genesis 1:27-30. Record your insights in the journaling section below.

Journaling My Insights . . .

_____

_____

_____

_____

_____

_____

_____

_____

_____

_____

_____

Hold To The Truth

"You shall not bear false witness against your neighbor." Exodus 20:16

This week's devotional theme:

God is Truth; any distortion of truth is abhorrent to Him.

God Is Truth

Remember the story of Ananias and Sapphira in Acts 5:1-10? It's a pretty scary account—a true, historical report of what happened in the early church at Jerusalem when two members of the church decided to lie.

They lied; they died.

Most of us, like Ananias and Sapphira, have no idea how intensely God hates dishonesty and how angry it makes Him. But we really shouldn't be surprised by God's reaction to dishonesty. We read in Scripture that truth is bound up in the very identity of God. Pontius Pilate was neither the first nor the last to ask, "What is truth?" But to him, and every other seeker, Jesus gives the final answer when He says, "I am the way, and the truth, and the life" (John 14:6).

"Don't gaze wistfully into space," we can almost hear Jesus say. "You won't find truth there. Nor will you find it deep within yourself. You'll only find truth in Me, for I am God, and God is Truth."

If God is Truth, then untruth—or dishonesty—is the antithesis of His being. It is contrary to His essence, and therefore utterly disgusting to Him. Falsehood cannot be tolerated by one who is intrinsically truthful.

Imagine an accomplished pianist—someone with perfect pitch—who is asked to perform on a piano that is woefully out of tune. Could she tolerate the grating disharmony for long? Or think of a skilled tradesman who views a poorly constructed building. Would uneven walls and unmatched trim bother him? Or put yourself in the place of a competent driver who is forced to "give the wheel" to a rookie. Could you sit back and quietly ignore the inexperienced driver's reckless techniques? Of course not! You couldn't tolerate that anymore than the pianist could tolerate the discordant piano, or the tradesman the shoddy workmanship. How then can we possibly expect the God of Truth to tolerate dishonesty?

We read in Proverbs that there are seven things which God hates: "Haughty eyes, a lying tongue, and hands that shed innocent blood, a heart that devises wicked plans, feet that run rapidly to evil, a false witness who utters lies, and one who spreads strife among brothers" (6:16-19). Two of these seven "abominations to Him" have to do with verbal dishonesty. It is to these sins that the ninth commandment speaks.

Be sure you're listening! In the next three days' worth of devotions, we will look at three ways to speak dishonestly or give false witness—lying, distortion, and exaggeration.

From the Father of Lies

Scripture tells us that the cesspool of evil which has flooded our planet began with a lie. When God placed Adam and Eve in the Garden of Eden, He told them not to eat of one particular tree: "For in the day that you eat from it, you shall surely die" (Gen. 2:17). But along came the serpent, who "was more crafty than any beast of the field which the Lord God had made"; and he said, "You surely shall not die! For God knows that in the day you eat from it your eyes will be opened, and you will be like God, knowing good and evil" (Gen. 3:1, 4-5). You know the rest of the story.

With his lie to Eve, Satan opened the floodgates of sin. Since then, he's been busy whispering lies into the hearts and minds of all God's children. And many of us get caught up in lies too—so caught up that we begin to adopt Satan's role. In theory we align ourselves with the God of truth, but in practice we wear the hat of a liar. Why do we do it?

Sometimes we lie to impress people. We claim to be bosom buddies with important people we barely know to boost our status. We lie when we fill out job applications to assure ourselves a position. We lie about past accomplishments to win acclaim.

Sometimes we lie to get revenge. We're angry with someone, so we make up stories to discredit him. Sometimes we lie to make a profit, as we discussed in the previous chapter. At other times we lie for convenience. We make excuses for not lending assistance to someone, when really, we simply don't want to get involved. We say we'll come to a party, when we have no intention of doing so. We just don't have the courage to say no.

At other times, we lie to escape punishment. I probably could fill a book with the lies people tell policemen to avoid getting traffic tickets. And what parent doesn't have a long list of "logical explanations" they've heard from a son or daughter who's missed curfew? Professors too spend untold hours listening to heartrending (though untrue) stories of why an assignment wasn't turned in on time.

Yes, we lie to impress, to get revenge, to make a profit, for convenience, and to escape punishment. In short, we lie a lot! Perhaps it's because we live in a society that minimizes the seriousness of lying. We've been conditioned to accept dishonesty with a sigh and a shrug of the shoulders.

The only sure way to snap this pattern is to declare all-out spiritual war. Every time the Holy Spirit convicts us about lying, we have to go right back to the person to whom we've lied and say, "I hate to admit this, but I lied to you. I didn't tell you the truth."

If you've ever done that, you know how humiliating the experience is. And you know that after doing it two or three times, you're going to think long and hard before you tell another lie.

Quote—Unquote

Distortion is a subtle form of lying. When we distort something, we don't utter bold-faced lies—we simply twist the truth. And one of the most common forms of distortion is misquoting.

It's so easy to destroy someone's reputation by misquoting his words. I've had people enter my office who were outraged over something I allegedly had said. Time and time again I've had to defend myself against misquotes. On occasion, I've even had to play a tape of a given message to prove I didn't say what I was reported to have said! And once, during a fund-raiser, I publicly announced that an anonymous donor had promised to match whatever sum of money we raised, up to $500,000. A rumor then began circulating in our community that an anonymous donor had given our church a large sum of money, and this donor had strong ties to a group considered to be a cult. You can see how ridiculous—and harmful—this distortion was. Not only were words put in my mouth, but conclusions were carelessly and erroneously drawn.

We distort the words of public personalities, neighbors, bosses, employees, friends, spouses, and even God. In Galatians, Paul warns about those who "want to distort the gospel of Christ" (1:7). It's one thing to distort the words of other human beings, but quite another to distort the words of God. Paul firmly says that individuals who do such a thing should "be accursed" (Gal. 1:8). Yet it does happen, repeatedly, when men and women mishandle truth. Mormons, Jehovah's Witnesses—and a host of others—twist the Scriptures to prove their points. They put together a mixture of truth, half-truth, and non-truth, and come up with their particular brand of religion.

But it's not only cultists who distort Scripture. Some Christians also twist the Word of God to suit their own ends. In some parts of this country, Christians defend segregation policies with the same Book that says, "There is neither Jew nor Greek, there is neither slave nor free man, there is neither male nor female; for you are all one in Christ Jesus" (Gal. 3:28).

Others use Jesus' own words to defend oppression policies. They claim that Jesus' statement, "the poor you have with you always" (Matt. 26:11), frees us from our responsibility to care for the needy and disadvantaged. They take one verse out of context and use it to nullify everything else that Jesus, and the whole of Scripture, say about the poor.

Whether we're using the words of other people, or the phrases of Scripture, we have to make every effort to use those words carefully and accurately. Misquoting and taking words out of context are nothing more than subtle lies. Don't do it!

Harmless Exaggeration?

Exaggeration is usually harmless, but it can be dangerous when used destructively. A husband sits in a counselor's office and says, "My wife never wants to attend important business functions with me." The wife says, "Well, you always humiliate me in public." The husband says, "You never express interest in my needs." The wife says, "You're always too busy to pay attention to me." Exaggeration polarizes a conversation and prohibits constructive communication.

Exaggeration even goes on in Christian circles. The music department at our church has a hard time selecting songs and choruses to use because so many of them exaggerate the truth. They present the Christian life as a bed of roses, filled with unending peace and happiness. They give the impression that Christians are somehow insulated from tragedy and disappointment, from problems and hardship. And that's a lie, a lie that unbelievers see through immediately.

Subtle lies like that even crop up now and then in testimonies. The young man who smoked an occasional joint in his pre-Christian days now claims he had a $400-a-day drug habit. Of course he's stretching the truth, but what a dramatic testimony of deliverance it makes! Or a woman confesses that before she became a Christian, she was lonely, empty, joyless, and insecure. But when she met Christ, He solved all her problems. Now she feels His presence all the time, is constantly filled with joy, and has the confidence to accomplish great things. God just keeps blessing and blessing!

Yes, God does keep blessing, but we lose our integrity as Christians when we overstate those blessings and portray a paradise that doesn't exist.

Fund-raising is another art that appears to benefit from the practice of exaggeration. Christian television personalities have been known to exaggerate their financial needs in order to move the masses. "This will be our last show," they cry, "unless you respond. Our bills must be paid within one week. If they're not, we're going off the air. It all depends on you." Sometimes, of course, such claims are legitimate; but in other instances, financial statements have proven them false. Organizations have pleaded financial despair when, in fact, they had millions of dollars in excess funds. How that must grieve the heart of God! Christian organizations have a duty to represent their financial standings honestly.

James tells us to "let [our] yes be yes, and [our] no, no" (5:12). Instead of getting all caught up in superlatives, we ought to take his advice and stick to the unblemished truth. We ought to speak in such a way that others can take our words at face value, confident that they accurately and objectively represent the truth.

Know the Truth

It's vitally important that we handle truths properly. It's also crucial that we handle Truth—the ultimate Truth of the Gospel—properly. But perhaps some of you who are reading this book have never heard the Truth of the Gospel of Jesus Christ. For that reason, I would like to present it here, in the form of four great truths that we all should know.

The first truth is that we all are moral failures. That's not my opinion, or even the opinion of the early church fathers. It's a truth established by God Himself (Rom. 3:23). And it's a truth we must come to grips with personally. No matter how "good" we appear in comparison to other people, we all fall dismally short of God's perfect moral standards.

As I mentioned in an earlier chapter, the summary of the Law is given in Mark's Gospel: "Hear, O Israel; the Lord our God is one Lord; and you shall love the Lord your God with all your heart, and with all your soul, and with all your mind, and with all your strength. . . . you shall love your neighbor as your-self" (12:29-31). After reading those words this morning, I had to get down on my knees and confess to God that I don't love Him the way I should. Nor do I obey His Word the way I ought to. It's the truth about all of us.

The second great truth is that someday we're going to stand in the blazing brilliance of God's holiness. Then all our shams and cover-ups will be seen for what they really are. Every little sin will stand out like a hideous stain. We may be able to hide the truth about ourselves now, but there will come a day when the condition of our souls will be painfully evident.

The third great truth is that people who have not repented will be doomed to an eternity in hell. Again, that's not my idea. And I wish I didn't have to talk about it. But the Bible says it's true. Unrepentant sinners will be separated from God forever and dwell in a place where evil will be unleashed in its full, unrestrained horror (Rev. 20:15).

The fourth great truth is that those who admit their sinfulness, and ask Jesus Christ to forgive them and become their Lord and Savior, will escape the judgment of hell and enter the kingdom of heaven.

Satan, of course, doesn't like to hear Truth. So he counters every word of Truth with lies—smooth-sounding ones, maybe—but lies, nonetheless. Satan told Eve that she would become like God, for example. Did she? He also said she'd never die. Did she?

The Bible says we have to admit the truth about ourselves—that we're sinners. Then we have to repent of our sin and reach out for the mercy and grace of Jesus Christ. That is our only hope.

Have you done that? If you haven't, please give careful thought to the Gospel of Truth. And then respond.

Week NINE REFLECTIONS

At the end of this week's readings, take some time to think about how these devotionals have affected you. For example, what spiritual insights have you gained? What practical applications have come to mind? How are your attitudes and/or actions likely to change as a result?

Use your responses as "grist" for your journal and as topics for prayer times with the Lord. In this way, you'll keep a record of your spiritual growth as God works out His will in your life.

For Personal Discovery:

1. What is one way you personally take care to be truthful, especially when others seem unconcerned with integrity?

2. Read Exodus 20:16. What does it mean to "bear false witness" (NASB)? What circumstances tempt you to lie?

3. Read Genesis 2:17 and 3:1, 4-5 concerning how Satan distorted God's truth in order to deceive Adam and Eve. Jesus calls Satan the "father of lies" (John 8:44). What does this name tell you about Satan?

4. There are two subtle forms of lying that often go unchecked: distortion and exaggeration. What examples of distortion and exaggeration have you witnessed?

5. Read Romans 7:14-25. Every one of us is tempted at times to mask our deceit. What does the passage in Romans teach you about the process of becoming a more truthful person?

6. If your family and close friends were asked to say how honest they thought you were, what would they say?

Personal Prayer Focus

- Give thanks to God that He Himself is Truth and that to know Him is to know truth.

- Knowing that dishonesty grieves God's heart, confess the times you have been careless in the way you handled the truth or were intentionally deceitful.

- Ask the Holy Spirit, the "Spirit of Truth," to bless you as you take steps to grow as a lover of truth.

- Meditate on these verses concerning "truth": Psalm 119:160; John 8:32; Romans 1:25; Philippians 1:18. Record your insights about these passages in the journaling section.

Journaling My Insights . . .

_____

_____

_____

_____

_____

_____

_____

_____

_____

_____

_____

Week
TEN

Crave
Contentment

"You shall not covet your neighbor's house; you shall not covet your neighbor's wife or his male servant or his female servant or his ox or his donkey or anything that belongs to your neighbor." Exodus 20:17

This week's devotional theme:

Coveting has wide-ranging effects on those who covet and on their relationships with God and other people.

What's Your Weak Spot?

Every year my dad bought a new car, put 40,000 miles on it without changing the oil or having it serviced, and then traded it back to the Ford dealer for a new one.

Every year the Ford dealer would say, "Well, Harold, can I talk you into some options this year?"

"Just a heater," Dad would say.

"Well, what about a color?" the dealer would ask.

"Cheap," Dad would answer. "Any color that's cheap. I like cheap colors."

Even Dad's wardrobe reflected his indifference to the material world. For one ten-year stretch, he wore nothing but black slacks and white shirts. And he bought his shoes by the case—all the same style and the same color. When people joked about it, he'd say, "It's one less decision I have to make. I reach into the closet and take the end shirt and the end pair of pants. No muss. No fuss. That's the way I like it." He was so disciplined, so disinterested in frills, so hard to excite . . . except when it came to Harley-Davidson motorcycles.

After he first got the thrill of the road on a big bike, within two years we had six of them in the garage—two big ones for Dad, one each for my brother and me, and models for my sisters!

One time a close friend of Dad's asked him if he could borrow his Harley to take on a short trip. Dad had a reputation for being generous with what he owned, so this man—a competent biker—didn't anticipate any problems. However, an uncomfortable silence met his request.

Finally Dad said, "You can sleep in my house, you can drive my car, you can sail my boat, you can fly my plane—but please, please don't ask to use my Harley!"

The Passion to Possess

I think most of us are a little like my dad. We have one little weak spot. Whether it's a motorcycle, a home, a boat, clothes, books, stamps, jewelry, furniture, art, music, horses, etc., most of us have a weakness that occasionally gives way to runaway desires. I don't think I've ever met anyone who doesn't have to struggle now and then to control the passion to possess something.

The tenth commandment warns us about this passion to possess. It tells us to be very careful about inordinate desires that encourage us to covet.

Coveting is an all-encompassing compulsion to possess something. It's not merely the act of admiring something. We certainly can appreciate an object for its beauty, workmanship, or function—and express that appreciation freely—without coveting it. But there's a big difference between saying, "I like that," and saying, "I have to own it." When we covet something, we decide we're not going to rest until we get it. What is it for you?

I Want It All!

Never in the history of civilization have people been as "pushed to possess" as we are. Marketing research is a billion-dollar-a-year business. Thousands of people in this country spend forty hours a week designing ways to trigger our buying mechanisms. They use music, slogans, sights, sounds, and colors to inflame our passion to possess. Often they attempt to stimulate fear, nostalgia, pride, sexual arousal, jealousy, or some other intense emotion. Their ultimate goal, though, is to impair our self-control just long enough for us to decide that we simply "must have" their product. They're trying to make us covet.

Advertisers are not, however, the only ones guilty of this ploy. Managers sometimes dangle attractive inducements in front of producers or salespeople in an effort to increase their output. "Just think," they say, "about that Caribbean cruise. Or that golfing vacation in Pebble Beach. Or that huge bonus." Some sales organizations even encourage people to hang color pictures of their dream possessions on their refrigerator, bulletin board, or bathroom mirror. Hopefully, these constant reminders will motivate them to sell more products.

Obviously, not all incentive programs are bad. But when their underlying motivation is to produce a fixation that causes an employee to sacrifice greater values for the sake of profits, those incentives are wrong. Any program, ploy, or advertisement that knowingly creates the climate for covetousness is a tool Satan can use to distract us from spiritual concerns.

Paul says, "If then you have been raised up with Christ, keep seeking the things above, where Christ is, seated at the right hand of God. Set your mind on the things above, not on the things that are on the earth" (Col. 3:1-2). *The Living Bible* says that if we really know the Lord we should "have as little desire for this world as a dead person does" (Col. 3:3, TLB). A familiar chorus tells us that if we "turn our eyes upon Jesus," the things of this world "will grow strangely dim."

Those concepts make sense to me. It seems reasonable to expect that those of us who truly know Christ as Lord and have our attention focused on Him should have a somewhat detached attitude toward material things. We should realize that though they're a necessary part of our earthly existence, they're not an ultimate value.

Why should we, who have been born again to spiritual life, allow ourselves to be controlled by runaway desires? Why should we fix our minds on things that will rust, rot, and depreciate? We are men and women created in the image of God; we've been called to be agents of reconciliation. We're created to accomplish eternal goals. When we fix our minds on transitory commodities and temporal goals, however, we live beneath our privilege.

I Want Yours!

In high school, I played basketball—not well, mind you, but very enthusiastically. I remember sitting on the bench, consciously wishing that our starting guard would get hurt so I could play. You probably can imagine what kind of relationship I had with that guy. I was envious of his abilities and his opportunities. Every time I looked at him, one thought went through my mind: I want your position!

Have you ever coveted another individual's job? Have you ever found yourself wishing that that person would miss an important deadline, or lose an account, so you could claim his position? Have you ever found yourself trying to make life miserable for her, or trying to sap her energy with inordinate demands? In other words, have you ever let the process of "wishing" for someone else's job push you into the process of "scheming" for it?

Have you ever coveted someone else's spouse? Have you ever made subtle plays for that person? Have you ever berated your own mate and fed your discontent by making insensitive comparisons? Have you ever taken covert action to undermine the solidity of a friend's marriage?

Have you ever heard selfish siblings count the days until a parent dies and frees up the inheritance? Have you ever seen them threaten their aging parents' dignity by making it clear that they value them only for the bank account they've promised to leave?

Coveting what belongs to another person is a serious offense on two counts. First, it indicates our lack of love for our neighbor, our relative, our friend, or whoever owns what we desire. When we place our affections on an inheritance, we remove our love from the person who's bequeathing it to us. When we see our neighbor's wife as the object of our desire, we begin to view our neighbor as the object of our disdain. When we scheme to get someone else's job, we reveal our calloused, insensitive heart. When we wish another person illness, injury, or bad fortune, we make it clear that the only person we care about is "number one"—ourselves. When we covet what belongs to someone else, we displace the owner. In our minds, we kick him out of the game, or out of the job, or out of the marriage.

Coveting another person's possessions also is serious because it unmasks our dissatisfaction with God's provision for us. In our hearts we say, "God, You've not been fair with me. I deserve a nicer husband, or a more lucrative position, or a bigger house, or higher status. You've shortchanged me. You owe me something better!" While we probably wouldn't verbalize those ideas, and may not even be consciously aware of them, they underlie every covetous thought, word, and action. They are, in fact, the basis of the covetous life. Will you join me in seeking to avoid that unhappy form of existence?

I Have Learned . . .

There is an alternative to the covetous life—the contented life.

Oh sure, you think, that's just what I want—to live like a lazy cow who lies on her belly and chews her cud. No action. No ambition. No drive. Sure. Let the world go by without me. I'm contented!

This may be a realistic description of the proverbial "contented cow," but it has nothing to do with an accurate picture of the contented lifestyle. Contentment is not passive. It's not the absence of ambition. And it's certainly not synonymous with laziness. It's simply a condition of the heart.

One can be relatively poor and be content. One can be very rich and be content. And one can fall somewhere in between and be content. Paul puts it like this:

"Not that I speak from want; for I have learned to be content in whatever circumstances I am. I know how to get along with humble means, and I also know how to live in prosperity; in any and every circumstance I have learned the secret of being filled and going hungry, both of having abundance and suffering need" (Phil. 4:11-12).

Contentment is a far cry from the covetous life. Unlike the covetous man who thinks God has dealt him an unfair hand, the contented man is grateful to God for whatever he has. He worships Him whether he's been blessed with little or with much. The contented man knows that if he has Christ as his Lord and Savior, he has everything he needs—and far more than he deserves.

I have only to flip back through the pages of this book to find out what I deserve. I've broken every one of the Ten Commandments to some degree, and because of that, I deserve the full measure of God's wrath. That's what I deserve. That, and nothing else.

But what has God given me? He's given me health, home, family, and friends. He's given me forgiveness, salvation, and the promise of life eternal. He's given me a ministry. He's given me His day-in and day-out presence. How dare I ask for more?

I ought to be asking myself why I have even that much. In view of who I am and how I've violated God, why has He blessed me with anything? The answer to that question is that we have a gracious God. When we're tempted to shake our fists at Him and say, "Why did You bless Harry or Mary more than You blessed me?" we'd better stop and repent. After all, He specializes in giving His children far more than they deserve.

Covetous or Contented?

The contented person not only has open hands, but open arms—arms that can embrace a brother or sister and rejoice in their good fortune. Imagine that your friend buys a new house, or your neighbor remodels her kitchen, or your coworker gets a promotion, or your brother-in-law hits it big with a shrewd investment. If you're a covetous person, you'll be filled with envy and anger. You won't be able to rejoice over another's good fortune. If you're a contented person, you'll say to your friend, "I sure hope you enjoy your new home!" And to your neighbor, "Hey, your new kitchen looks great!" And to your coworker, "Best of luck in your new position!" And to your brother-in-law, "How exciting! I'm thrilled for you!"

The contented person is free to rejoice when another gains—and to weep when another loses. Paul said, "And if one member suffers, all the members suffer with it; if one member is honored, all the members rejoice with it" (1 Cor. 12:26). When the basketball star whose position you want to play gets injured, do you rejoice in your "lucky break," or do you try to feel the anguish of his disappointment? When an acquaintance loses his business, do you gloat over your "good management skills," or do you try to think of ways to help him? Do you laugh at the woman who weeps, or do you weep with her?

The covetous person dreams of taking. The contented person dreams of sharing. The covetous one clutches all he has with a tight fist, in fear of others. The contented one holds what she has with open hands, and reaches out to embrace others.

O that we would all learn the joy of the contented life. We're physical, material beings, so we'll always have physical, material needs. But those of us who keep those needs in perspective, who fix our minds on Jesus Christ, and who accept His gifts with grateful hearts, can experience the joy of the contented life.

Paul tells us that "the Law has become our tutor to lead us to Christ, that we may be justified by faith" (Gal. 3:24). In other words, the Law points out our sin, so that we can see our need for a Savior. If reading this book has been a difficult and frustrating experience for you, it may be that the Law has succeeded in doing exactly what it's supposed to do—it's forced you down on your knees in humble repentance.

If that's been true for you, don't hesitate. Jesus is only a prayer away. If you repent of your sin right now, He'll forgive you, enter your life, and begin a good work in you that will continue for the rest of your life. His Holy Spirit will so transform you that in a few years, you'll look back and say, "I'm a different person than I used to be. I still violate God's laws now and then, but I know I'm heading in the right direction. I'm changing. I'm growing. And I'm liberated at last!"

Week TEN REFLECTIONS

At the end of this week's readings, take some time to think about how these devotionals have affected you. For example, what spiritual insights have you gained? What practical applications have come to mind? How are your attitudes and/or actions likely to change as a result?

Use your responses as "grist" for your journal and as topics for prayer times with the Lord. In this way, you'll keep a record of your spiritual growth as God works out His will in your life.

For Personal Discovery:

1. When have you wanted someone else's job, spouse, car, etc.? Were you aware, at that time, that you were coveting? What are your greatest material passions in life?

2. Read Exodus 20:17. What does it mean to "covet" something or someone? What are some ways that our society encourages you to covet?

3. How might you be causing people to covet by the way you motivate them? (Example: You want your high school child to study more, so you say to him, "Good grades, good college, good job, nice house all go together. So study up!")

4. Read Ecclesiastes 4:4. How can this observation challenge you to rethink the way you conduct your business and the way you relate to others?

5. We often hear about a person's "right" to certain possessions. These rights may give people a sense of dignity. But when we act like we have a *right* to have certain things or to be *like* someone else, we are, in effect, telling God that He owes us. What, if anything, do you think God owes you?

Personal Prayer Focus

- In your prayer time this week, meditate on the teachings found in Colossians 3:1-4 and Philippians 4:11-12.

- Read Luke 10:18-20 aloud. Think about how your relationship with the living God changes emphasis from what you do to who you are in Him.

- End your time of prayer by reading Job 1:1 aloud. Give thanks to God for the liberating truth of this verse.

Journaling My Insights . . .

_____

_____

_____

_____

_____

_____

_____

_____

_____

_____

_____

_____

_____